HIGHER GROUND

I'm pressing on the upward way,
New heights I'm gaining every day;
Still praying as I onward bound
'Lord, plant my feet on higher ground.'

My heart has no desire to stay
Where doubts arise and fears dismay.
Tho' some may dwell where these abound,
My prayer, my aim is higher ground.

I want to live above the world,
Tho' Satan's darts at me are hurled;
For faith has caught the joyful sound,
The song of saints on higher ground.

I want to scale the utmost height,
And catch a gleam of glory bright;
But still I'll pray till heav'n I've found
'Lord, lead me on to higher ground.'

Lord, lift me up and let me stand,
By faith, on heaven's table-land,
A higher plane than I have found,
Lord, plant my feet on higher ground.

Johnson Oatman, Jnr

Higher Ground

Insights from the Psalms of Ascent
(Psalms 120-134)

RT Kendall

Christian Focus Publications

© 1995 RT Kendall
ISBN 1-85792-158-5

Published by
Christian Focus Publications Ltd.
Geanies House, Fearn, Ross-shire,
IV20 1TW, Scotland, Great Britain

Printed and bound in Great Britain by
Cox & Wyman Ltd, Reading, Berkshire

Cover design by Donna Macleod

Contents

To
Robert and Beth

PREFACE

Every minister needs a friend – probably another minister. I have such a friend – Robert Amess, pastor of Duke Street Baptist Church in Richmond, Surrey.

Robert and I try to see each other for coffee or lunch two or three times a month, and I think I can safely say we need each other. 'Iron sharpens iron', and I can say that Robert does this for me!

A couple of years ago he came in to see me with a 'word from the Lord'. This is unlike Robert, but he was serious. I said, 'What is it?' He said, 'I know what you should preach on for your next series.' 'Really?' 'Yes.' 'Then tell me – quick.'

He then said that he had been looking at the Psalms of Ascent, Psalms 120 to 134, and it burned on his heart that I should preach on these. He then promised to give me a book on the subject, which he later did. As it turns out, the book was only of minimal value, but his suggestion burned in my own heart and it turns out that I believe Robert was really right to urge me to preach on the Psalms of Ascent.

Christian Focus kindly asked that this become a book. It is presented herewith. I want to thank

Mrs Alison Linnell for editing these sermons, which were preached between September 1993 and January 1994. As always, I am grateful to Mr Malcolm Maclean, my editor with Christian Focus.

But when it came to the dedication, there was only one person that would come to my mind – that is Robert. But I want to add his beloved wife Beth, close friends of Louise and me.

R.T. Kendall
June 1995

Introduction

C. S. Lewis reminds us that psalms are poems intended to be sung. They are not doctrinal treatises nor even sermons.

The Psalms are primarily for believers. They were written to express to God how we feel. The wonderful thing about our relationship with God is that we can tell him how we feel. He knows how we feel anyway, but he likes it when we express what is in our hearts. The Psalms record many of the very different experiences of God's people, and they are of immense help to us today, for we will face similar problems and enjoy similar blessings. Therefore it is important that we read the Psalms often.

I can't begin to tell you what the Psalms mean to me. I would rather read the Psalms than almost any other part of the Bible. I use Robert Murray McCheyne's Bible reading plan that guides me to read a psalm regularly. When I am not reading a psalm I really feel deprived because I love to live in the Psalms.

The fifteen psalms from 120 to 134 are called *songs of ascents*. The word 'ascent' comes from a Hebrew word which means *going up*. It seems that these particular psalms were sung by pilgrims on their way to Jerusalem to keep the annual feasts. No matter where they journeyed from, they had to go up because Jerusalem is 2,500 feet above sea level. There were three festivals each year and the Jews would sing these psalms as they ascended to Jerusalem.

In this book I do not intend to give a full exposition of each psalm. Rather I will take one leading thought from each psalm which I believe is relevant to situations Christians face today. So, for example, from Psalm 120, the thought is the *tongue*; from Psalm 121, it is *help*; from Psalm 122, it is *Jerusalem*; from Psalm 123, it is *mercy*. Not all of these psalms can be summarized with one word, but our aim is to look for the obvious theme or themes that will hold the particular psalm together.

As the ancient pilgrim went up to Jerusalem I pray that your heart will be lifted as these marvellous psalms are briefly explored.

1

Psalm 120

How God gets our attention

I call on the LORD in my distress,
    and he answers me.
  Save me, O LORD, from lying lips
    and from deceitful tongues.
  What will he do to you,
    and what more besides, O deceitful tongue?
  He will punish you with a warrior's sharp arrows,
    with burning coals of the broom tree.
  Woe to me that I dwell in Meshech,
    that I live among the tents of Kedar!
  Too long have I lived
    among those who hate peace.
  I am a man of peace;
    but when I speak, they are for war.

I read through the Psalms at least twice a year. Psalm 120 always seems like a breath of fresh air after the 176 verses of Psalm 119. Don't get me wrong, I love Psalm 119, but it is so intense and long. Then comes Psalm 120.

Has God ever got your attention? To my mind, that is what this psalm is about. What did God have to do to get your attention? There are many ways God can use.

There are those who can talk about the beauty of Jesus, and the beauty of Jesus will make unbelievers want to become Christians. There are those who are gifted in preaching the gospel. The Negro slaves in Mississippi, Alabama and Georgia were won by the thought of heaven.

God has also used preaching on hell to get some people's attention.

I suspect that this generation rarely hears the preaching of hell under the power of the Holy Spirit. I have preached on the subject, and I don't want to doubt that God could have used me. We have no idea what it would be like were God to own a particular message on hell. When John the Baptist preached, 'Flee from the wrath to come', people were scared out of their minds! God used him.

But what I want to stress is that God can use many different ways to get our attention.

Psalm 120 gives us a number of examples of

ways that God uses. In this case they are all various forms of distress.

'I call on the LORD in my distress' (verse 1). Are you in distress at the moment? Distress can be caused by guilt, or by grief; it can be the result of pressure at work. It could be that you are in distress because of an examination outcome, or preparation for it.

Whatever the cause, perhaps you have never realized that God has permitted the distress and, because you lack this perspective, you fear that you will break under the strain. But God is saying, 'I am behind all that is going on right now. I am the architect of the distress. And do you know why? It is the only way I could get your attention.'

Lying lips and deceitful tongues
One form of distress that God uses to get our attention is caused by *the deceit of others*: 'Save me, O LORD, from lying lips and from deceitful tongues' (verse 2). This was the origin of the psalmist's distress, he had been criticized unfairly.

I wonder if this is close to where you are. Maybe part of the reason you are in distress is that you have been criticised, and it hurts. Criticism is painful, even if it is true. In fact, sometimes the criticism that we don't want to hear is so hard to take because it is true. If people begin a sentence with 'I say this in love', watch out! Of course, 'faithful are the wounds of a friend' (Proverbs 27:6). But the psalmist was the victim of a deceitful tongue. Have you ever known the pain of finding out that someone, who seemed to be a friend, was insincere? If so, then you have suffered the pain of being deceived.

But even that doesn't quite express all the meaning. The psalmist had either been lied *to* or lied *about*. What is a lie? A lie is the postponement of the truth that will come out. I mention this to encourage anybody who has been lied about, and the lie has been believed. It is only a matter of time before the truth will come out. I guarantee it.

It can be very painful, however, during that time of postponement. Maybe that's where you are. Perhaps you have lost your job because someone lied about you; perhaps you have lost a friendship because something was said that wasn't true; perhaps you have lost influence because somebody lied about you, and there is not a thing you can do to defend yourself. Not that you should, but the temptation is there to put the record straight. But I promise you, if you have been lied about, one day the truth will come out, although you may have to wait a while.

Remember who is on your side: God. God is truth, it is impossible for him to lie (Hebrews 6:18). When anybody says anything about you that is not true, God doesn't like it. The day is coming when

God will clear not only his own name, but your name too.

Why would this particular source of distress be in a psalm of ascent? I believe the answer is this: bad things often happen when something good is supposed to happen. The highlights of the year for the Jews were the times when they went up to the feasts in Jerusalem. But there were those, rejoicing on their way to the feasts, who were brought right down because of a deceitful tongue. Has something similar ever happened to you? For example, just as you are getting ready to go to church, have you been involved in an argument in the house; an argument with your husband or with your wife?

Do you see how often the tongue interferes with something good? When the tongue interferes with something good, we often ask, 'Is this of God, or is it of the devil?' The answer is that it could be the devil and that God is using the devil as his instrument. The devil can do nothing without God's permission. God allows the devil to go so far but no further.

What consolation is there if someone lies about you? It is that God doesn't like it, and he will step in:

What will he [God] do to you,
    and what more besides, O deceitful tongue?

> He will punish you with a warrior's
>   sharp arrows,
>   with burning coals of the broom tree
>   (verses 3-4).

Let me tell you what to do if you have been lied to, or lied about. Here's your opportunity for great strength of character. Let God handle it. He likes that. He likes it when we believe in him so much that we let him handle things for us. But he doesn't like it when we try to handle things ourselves because he is the great vindicator who wants to clear your name.

'Woe to me ...'

Further on in this psalm we find another reason for distress; the pilgrims were *displaced*. Look at verse 5: 'Woe to me that I dwell in Meshech, that I live among the tents of Kedar!' Meshech and Kedar symbolize places where we do not like to have to live. Are you living in the 'wrong' place? Perhaps you are feeling a little sorry for yourself. But maybe God has put you there so that you will value what really matters, such as going up to Zion to worship God. Because of an unhappy situation, where things just aren't the way you would like them to be, God gets your attention.

But there is more in this. The distress was obviously caused by *danger*, because Meshech and

Kedar also symbolize places of danger. Kedar, for example, refers to the Bedouins who were a perpetual problem to the travellers. Are you one of those people who enjoys living on the edge of danger, so you sail close to the wind, but now find yourself in trouble?

Yet another part of the distress comes out in verse 6, *delay*: 'Too long have I lived among those who hate peace.' Perhaps your distress is because of a prolonged situation. You have waited and waited for the situation to change. In reality, however, all this time perhaps God has been waiting for you to turn to him.

The last way revealed in this psalm by which God gets our attention is through *discord*: 'I am a man of peace; but when I speak, they are for war' (verse 7). Are you in such a situation *of discord*? Perhaps your marriage is on the rocks, perhaps you are living somewhere where there is nothing but tension. God can use discord to get your attention.

It is important that we respond consciously and positively to God's effort to get our attention. The psalmist responded, for he said, 'I call on the LORD in my distress' (verse 1), this stress being caused by tension around him. What makes for peace is when we come to terms with the fact that the problem is not merely the situation but our reaction to the situation. In the midst of tension do we do the things that make for peace (Romans 14:19)? That means I will be a peacemaker *externally*: with reference to those around me (Matthew 5:9); literally doing and saying things that lead to another's peace. A man of peace thus will defuse heated situations, not adding to their misery. Such a man can do this because *internally* he has discovered and experienced 'perfect peace' (Isaiah 26:3). It is called the 'peace of God, which transcends all understanding' (Philippians 4:7). He did what gave him inner peace.

That is what the psalmist meant. But it is often a lonely experience. So often 'they are for war' (Psalm 120:7). Such loneliness is yet another way God gets our attention.

2

Psalm 121

The greatest fringe benefit of all

I lift up my eyes to the hills —
  where does my help come from?
My help comes from the LORD,
  the Maker of heaven and earth.
He will not let your foot slip —
  he who watches over you will not slumber;
 indeed, he who watches over Israel
  will neither slumber nor sleep.
The LORD watches over you —
  the LORD is your shade at your right hand;
 the sun will not harm you by day,
  nor the moon by night.
The LORD will keep you from all harm —
  he will watch over your life;
the LORD will watch over your coming and going
both now and for evermore.

Psalm 121 is probably the best known of the songs of ascent. However, one of the effects of modern versions of the Bible is that we have to rethink and reinterpret long-held opinions about the meaning of well-known Scripture sections. It also destroys a lot of old sermons!

In the Authorized Version, verse 1 reads: 'I will lift up mine eyes unto the hills, from whence cometh my help.' There have been many sermons preached on how, by looking to the hills, one gets help from the Lord. There were many times in ancient Israelite history when God did special things on mountains.

I once preached on Psalm 121 and pointed out the various mountains in the Bible where God met with his people: Mount Sinai, Mount Carmel, the Mount of Transfiguration, the Mount of Olives, and lastly Mount Calvary. The Authorized Version gives the impression that looking to the hills is a good thing. But all of the modern versions differ from it.

In the New International Version, verse 1 reads: 'I lift up my eyes to the hills – where does my help come from?' This led me to double-check the original language, to ask why there is a question mark. It seems that instead of looking to the hills for help, it is likely the psalmist had the very opposite in mind. The hills did not indicate the places where God met with his people, rather they were locations of idolatry where sacrifices were made to the god, Baal.

I lift up my eyes to the hills

Why did the psalmist say these words? Firstly, it is possible that in a moment of *temptation* he was thinking, 'Shall I look to the hills like so many others are doing?' Those who were worshipping Baal were increasing in number rapidly. Many were looking to the hills for help, so the psalmist pauses and asks: 'Where does my help come from?' But he realizes his help does not come from the hills. Quite the opposite, in fact; his help comes from the Lord.

Secondly, it is possible that the writer was referring to the *tradition* of looking to mountains. There were those who, by looking to the mountains in the direction of Jerusalem, had a good feeling. For 'the mountains surround Jerusalem' (Psalm 125:2).

Thirdly, when the travellers were looking to the hills, they might have thought of *togetherness*. They were going to Jerusalem for the feasts, and they would be meeting people whom they hadn't seen for a long time.

In any case, whether they were looking because of temptation, or because of tradition, or because of togetherness, the psalmist stops and says, 'My help comes from the LORD.' Not mountains.

As I said, the hills could well have symbolized temptation. Have you been wrestling with a problem of temptation from a certain direction, and you know by looking in that direction, you are looking where temptation will be? Do you know the best way to prevent yourself falling into sin? It is to keep from falling into temptation. Most of us have a fairly shrewd idea of what will tempt us. What may be my weakness may not be yours, and what may be yours may not be mine. But we all have an idea where our weak spot is.

Have you been looking in the direction of temptation? Are you at this moment planning to be at a certain place at a certain time? You know that you are going to go into a place where you will be tempted. Maybe you are involved in something that is wrong, and if you were to be found out you would be destroyed. But you keep on going in the same direction. If you are involved in anything that is questionable, break it off now!

Perhaps your temptation is very similar to that which some believe the hills symbolized; the temptation of idolatry. Baal-worship was tantamount to worshipping the devil. Do you know that the devil has strange ways of coming into our lives? Such ways include astrology or horoscopes. These even appear on early morning television. If you are watching such programmes, do you listen to the horoscopes? Do you read your star signs in the

newspaper? Don't ever think, not even out of curi-
osity, about looking at your star sign or reading an
astrology chart. If you are playing around with a
good luck charm, stop it!

Perhaps you are looking to tradition for help. I
think England is the most traditional country in
the world. I sometimes think Westminster Chapel
is the most traditional church in England. Maybe
you like tradition. But you can be so tied up in
tradition that you never reach the Lord. You can
come to church and get a good feeling. You like
the organ, you like the architecture. But that is just
looking to the hills for reasons of tradition. Your
good feeling may not be from the Lord at all.

The greatest fringe benefit of all

This is the theme from Psalm 121 on which I want
to focus. Why do I want to deal with this subject?
Let me ask you this question: Why did you become a Christian? The primary reason surely is so
that you will go to heaven when you die. The modern church appears largely to have forgotten that
people become Christians for the reason that the
Bible gives. The reason why Jesus died on the cross
is summed up in John 3:16 (which Martin Luther
called 'the Bible in a nutshell'): 'For God so loved
the world that he gave his one and only Son, that
whoever believes in him shall not perish, but have
eternal life.'

Jesus bore the wrath of God in our place. The day will come when Jesus, as judge, will say to those who do not know God, 'Depart from me, you who are cursed, into eternal fire' (Matthew 25:41). Because the fires of hell do not satisfy the justice of God, they burn for ever. But the blood shed by Jesus Christ of Nazareth satisfied God's justice completely. This is what assures us of a home in heaven. This is the reason to be a Christian.

The eternal perspective is not, however, the only reason to become a Christian. What salvation will do for us in this life can be underestimated, but the fact is there are many fringe benefits of being a Christian. For example, the promise that God will supply all our needs (Philippians 4:19). Or the promise that by delighting in the Lord we will have the desire of our heart (Psalm 37:4). Or the promise that no good thing will be withheld from those whose walk is blameless (Psalm 84:11). For that matter, where are these promises found? In the Bible, God's gift to the believer – what a wonderful fringe benefit! Psalm 121 suggests even more fringe benefits.

The main fringe benefit of being a Christian is found in verse 5: 'The LORD watches over you – the LORD is your shade at your right hand.' Do you know what that tells me? It assures me of God's very presence. The psalmist said in Psalm 16:8: 'Because he is at my right hand, I shall not be shaken.' This means that God promises us *himself*. Not only are we assured of going to heaven, but the greatest thing of all is that Jesus says to us, 'You've got me! I am with you always, even to the end. I will never leave you nor forsake you.' There is nothing more wonderful than knowing that we have him.

What does that mean?

First of all, it means *help*: 'My help comes from the LORD, the maker of heaven and earth' (verse 1). There have been times in my life when I really do not know what I would have done without the Lord. He has a way of slipping alongside me at the moment when I think I can't go on. He is never too late, never too early, but always just on time.

The psalmist says in verse 3, 'He will not let your foot slip – he who watches over you will not slumber.' Now this was an implicit put-down of Baal.

Remember when Elijah confronted the prophets of Baal on Mount Carmel (1 Kings 18). He challenged them to prove whose God was the true God, the God who answered by fire. When the prophets of Baal shouted to their god, there was no response. Elijah began to taunt them and suggested that Baal was sleeping. It was a put-down of the false god.

What does the psalmist say? His God will neither slumber nor sleep.

Not only will we get God's help if we are Christians, but we have his *continual attention*. He watches over us. The word 'watch' is used several times in this psalm. God watches over our life, our comings and goings.

Have you ever been in a situation where you have thought, 'I wish somebody could see what is happening to me right now'? Or maybe something good has happened to you but there is nobody to share it with.

It is the most wonderful thing to realize that our heavenly Father is there. And there will come a time, if you develop the relationship with him that is available to you, when his attention will mean more to you than anything.

One of the most moving words in all the Bible is in Genesis 16, when Hagar looked up to heaven and said, 'You are the God who sees me' (verse 13).

I know what it is like to be in a situation where you wonder, 'Will anybody understand? Will anybody know what I am going through?', and suddenly God says, 'I know.' Remember the words of the old spiritual: 'Nobody knows the troubles I've seen, nobody knows but Jesus.' If *he* knows, we can live with it. What God is saying is that he wants the kind of relationship with us where his approval will mean everything to us.

The travellers on their way to Jerusalem faced

possible harm from three areas: they could step on a stone and sprain an ankle, they could suffer from sunstroke or they could be affected by moonstroke – lunacy. (Lunacy is so called, because people of ancient times believed the moon could cause them to lose their mental faculties.) But the psalmist says: 'The sun will not harm you by day, nor the moon by night.'

However, when the psalmist says, 'He will not let your foot slip,' it is not an absolute promise that just because you have become a Christian, nothing bad will ever happen to you again. This is the folly of the 'Health and Wealth' gospel that is popular across the Atlantic. We will come back to this distortion of the gospel in chapter 9 when we look at Psalm 128. For the moment, however, it will suffice to say that the Bible does not promise us that.

It could be that God will let your foot slip. He may let you fall into temptation and into sin. It has happened. But it doesn't need to happen. So what do you do?

Because the honour of God is at stake, you should come before God, sometimes to fast and pray that his honour will be protected. What the psalmist does is to show that whatever happens to us, happens by God's permission, even if it seems to be negative.

The greatest fringe benefit of belonging to the

Lord is knowing you have him now. True, you know that you will go to heaven when you die. But when you became a Christian God didn't just shake your hand and say, 'Well done, see you in heaven!' No, he says, 'I will be with you. I will see everything that is going on; your coming and your going, both now and ever more.'

3

Psalm 122

Jerusalem, yesterday, today and forever

I rejoiced with those who said to me,
  'Let us go to the house of the LORD.'
Our feet are standing
  in your gates, O Jerusalem.
Jerusalem is built like a city
  that is closely compacted together.
That is where the tribes go up,
  the tribes of the LORD,
to praise the name of the LORD
  according to the statute given to Israel.
There the thrones for judgment stand,
  the thrones of the house of David.
Pray for the peace of Jerusalem:
  'May those who love you be secure.
May there be peace within your walls
  and security within your citadels.'
For the sake of my brothers and friends,
  I will say, 'Peace be within you.'
For the sake of the house of the LORD our God,
  I will seek your prosperity.

We have seen how the travellers sang these psalms of ascent on their way up to Jerusalem. Psalm 122, however, would appear to have been sung on the steps of the temple:

> I rejoiced with those who said to me,
>> 'Let us go to the house of the LORD.'
> Our feet are standing
>> in your gates, O Jerusalem.

It is one thing to look forward to something and quite another when it is just about to happen. Expectancy is then higher than ever. At the temple the pilgrims sang with joy, for they were so glad to be there. They actually began to sing *to* Jerusalem, to sing *to* the city.

The heading of this psalm indicates that it was composed by David. Some commentators have a problem with this because there was not a temple in Jerusalem when David was king. So David couldn't have been referring to the temple when he mentioned the house of the Lord. C. H. Spurgeon suggested that David was speaking prophetically, for he knew the day was coming when the temple would be built by his son, Solomon. David was rejoicing in advance.

Do you know what it is to love a city so much that you want to sing *to* it? I don't mean sing *about* it. Do you love your city that much? I don't know of anybody who loves London enough to want to sing to it. I don't know of any New Yorker who wants to sing to New York! But Jerusalem was different. It is impossible to exaggerate the affection, not just nostalgia, that Israelis felt and feel to this day about the city of Jerusalem. In this psalm about Jerusalem there are these words in verse 6: 'Pray for the peace of Jerusalem.' When was the last time you prayed for the peace of Jerusalem?

Pray for the peace of Jerusalem
In this chapter I want to suggest several reasons why we should pray in this way.

The first reason is for its *history*. If you are converted, one of the things you are going to be interested in is a history that never gripped you before. You have become a member of a new family: the Christian church. I do not mean a literal building, for the church is a people. You find that your new family has a history.

David was the one who conquered the city of Jerusalem and it became known as the city of David. Jerusalem had been regarded as the one place nobody could penetrate. But David did.

Now Jerusalem did not belong to any of the twelve tribes of Israel. David himself was of the tribe of Judah, and, prior to conquering Jerusalem, had made Hebron his capital. Hebron was located in the territory allocated to Judah, and many peo-

ple would have suspected that it was for this reason it was chosen. David's choice of city might
not have excited people, but it could have caused
division. Jerusalem, however, belonged to nobody,
so when David conquered it, there was no rival
spirit, no competition between cities. Jerusalem
became the capital, and throughout its history it
was special.

There is another reason why we should be interested in Jerusalem and that is because of its
heritage. God chose Jerusalem (Zechariah 3:2).
Now we know that God's choosing is never a last-
minute decision. God chooses from the beginning
and so, in his providence, when David was conquering Jerusalem, he was conquering a city that
had been saved for Israel to be their capital. So the
fact that God himself chose the city should make
you interested in it.

After anyone is converted, it is only a matter of
time before they will discover the family secret,
which is that God chose them before they were
born, before the creation of the world. What an
encouragement this is to those who have had no
sense of identity! Before I was born, before my
parents were born, from before the creation of the
world, *God loved me*!

God chose Jerusalem. What a heritage!

Thirdly we should pray for the peace of Jerusalem because of the *hostility* that is and has been

directed at it. The name 'Jerusalem' means 'City of peace', but no city in the world has so belied its name. Sadly, in its long history, Jerusalem has known little or nothing of peace. There is a kind of jealousy that exceeds all other jealousies, and that's the jealousy people will have towards anything that God chooses. God chose Jerusalem and ordained it as the place where his honour would dwell – therefore people hated Jerusalem.

History records at least three-dozen sieges of Jerusalem. Some are recorded in the Bible, some have occurred since the Bible was written. For example, Jerusalem was besieged by the king of Egypt, by the king of Syria, by Sennacherib, king of Assyria, by Nebuchadnezzar, king of Babylon, by the Roman general Titus in 70 AD, and afterwards by Muslims and Crusaders. In modern times, Britain wrested it from the Turks; the Israelis wrested it from Jordan.

God ordained Jesus Christ to be the Saviour of the world. As a result people hated Jesus Christ. If you are identified with Jesus Christ, don't expect everybody to clap their hands and rejoice and congratulate you. Instead, you will find that they will distance themselves from you, and think there is something wrong with you. You will feel their hostility.

Jesus said, 'Do not suppose that I have come to bring peace to the earth.' He said, 'I have come to create division.' Don't ask why, but he said, 'I have come to turn a man against his father, a daughter against her mother, a daughter-in-law against her mother-in-law' (see Matthew 10:34-37). When a person is converted, it is supernatural. Nobody knows why in one family, one person will be converted and another will not. There is nothing more heartbreaking than this. All that believers can do is to pray earnestly for God to save their unconverted relatives.

But there is a fourth reason why we should pray for Jerusalem: it is called the *Holy City* (Nehemiah 11:1), that is, it is set apart. It was to be holy because it should reflect the character of God – who is holy (Leviticus 11:44; 1 Peter 1:16). God is pure, wholly other – that is, unlike anyone or anything here below. Therefore as God is to be revered so too the city of his choice was to be regarded as sacred. But today Jerusalem is 'holy' to three great religions: to Jews, to Christians and to Muslims. Each religion has holy sites in Jerusalem.

The Muslims built the Dome of the Rock on the place where the temple of Solomon had been built, for they believe that Mohammed ascended from this area.

Jews revere the Western Wall, all that remains of Herod's temple. There some pray for the coming of Messiah.

Christians have special regard for the traditional locations of the Garden of Gethsemane and for Calvary, as well as what lies within the Ancient City.

So Jerusalem is a divided city. More than ever, we can see the relevance of praying for Jerusalem. But to Christians it is special because so much activity took place there.

It was outside the city gates that Jesus died on the cross. Because he died on that cross, all of our sins were charged to him. And if we believe in Jesus, God does not declare us guilty any more. When he shed his blood, that blood satisfied God's justice. Knowing that we are right with God is the most wonderful feeling in the world. We may face hatred and persecution, but we can still have the sense that there is peace between us and God.

There is a fifth reason why Jerusalem is special; because it is *home*. It is home, because we reach a place in the New Testament where Jerusalem takes on a different meaning. In Galatians 5:26, we are told about the Jerusalem which is in heaven, the Jerusalem that is above. The name Jerusalem continues right on into the future, it is the name given to the home of Christians throughout eternity. On the isle of Patmos, John had a vision and 'saw the Holy City, the new Jerusalem, coming down out of heaven from God' (Revelation 21:2). It is the place where God will wipe away all tears.

One day God will clear his name. He will answer all our questions. Are you looking forward to that? God is looking forward to that. And it is going to take place in the new Jerusalem.

The apostle Paul said, 'Our citizenship is in heaven.'

4

Psalm 123

Not getting what you deserve

I lift up my eyes to you,
   to you whose throne is in heaven.
As the eyes of slaves look to the hand of
                              their master,
   as the eyes of a maid look to the hand of
                              her mistress,
so our eyes look to the Lord our God,
   till he shows us his mercy.
Have mercy on us, O Lord, have mercy on us,
   for we have endured much contempt.
We have endured much ridicule from the proud,
   much contempt from the arrogant.

Martin Luther said that this particular psalm shows that the force of prayer consists not in *many* words, but in *fervency* of spirit. Every prayer is long enough, if it is fervent.

Each of the previous psalms of ascent has been characterized by an operative word: in Psalm 120 it was the *tongue*; in Psalm 121 it was *help;* in Psalm 122 it was *Jerusalem*. In Psalm 123 the operative word is *mercy*:

> As the eyes of slaves look to the hand of
> > their master,
> > as the eyes of a maid look to the hand of her
> > > mistress,
> so our eyes look to the LORD our God,
> > till he shows us his mercy.
> Have mercy on us, O LORD,
> > have mercy on us ...   (verses 2-3).

When was the last time you asked another person for *mercy*? I may ask a friend for a favour, but if I ever ask him for mercy, he will know that I am in bad shape. I would hate to think that I might ever be so desperate that I would need to ask for mercy from another person.

Have you ever asked God for mercy? Have you ever come to that point where you have realized that God doesn't owe you a favour? He doesn't owe you an explanation, rather what you need is mercy.

The writer of this psalm (we don't know who it was) understood that God can give or withhold mercy. The person who has realized this comes to know God in an altogether new way. So the psalm was written by one who understood God.

It was written by one who also understood himself. He had come to terms with what he was like. He realized he had no right to snap his fingers and say, 'God, you have to do this!' He knew that God doesn't have to do anything. Therefore he said, 'We will just look to God. We will wait for him. As the eyes of slaves look to the hands of their master, as the eyes of a maid look to the hands of her mistress, so our eyes look to the Lord.'

In the chapter on Psalm 121, we saw that the psalmist had been considering looking to the hills for help. But he had stopped and said, 'My help doesn't come from the hills, it comes from the Lord.' In Psalm 123, the writer intends to keep looking to and waiting for the Lord to come in mercy.

Have you ever talked to God like that? If you haven't, you are not a Christian. A Christian is a person who has come to realize that he has no bargaining power. He sees himself as having sinned against God, offended his holiness, broken his law, and shown contempt for his word. When a person realizes that he is a sinner, all he can do is ask for mercy.

What is mercy?

One definition of mercy is 'refraining from inflicting punishment or pain on an offender or enemy who is in one's power'. Here is a person who has the right to punish and also the power to do so. He has the right to punish, because the offender deserves justice, and deserves to be punished. Mercy occurs when the person who could punish shows leniency instead. In short, God's mercy is not getting what we, as sinners, deserve.

One evening, some years ago, I was driving in Miami Beach. As I approached a traffic light, I was doing 35 miles per hour. Suddenly the green light turned yellow, and I went through on the red light. I looked in my mirror and there was a blue light, going off and on!

There was a sinking feeling in my stomach! And the trouble was, I knew what I had done! I stopped my car and walked back to the police car. I could tell the officer knew that I knew what I had done.

I just looked at him and said, 'I hope you won't give me a ticket.'

'Why?' he asked.

'I would appreciate it!' I said.

He said, 'You went through a red light, and you ask me not to give you a ticket! Give me one reason why I shouldn't give you a ticket?'

I said, 'I live in Fort Lauderdale, I believe the lights in Fort Lauderdale stay yellow just a little longer!' At that the officer rolled his eyes heaven-ward!

'You know,' he said, 'I have given out nineteen tickets today and I want twenty so I can go home!' A policeman like that has goals.

I looked at him and pleaded, 'Please don't give me a ticket!'

He said, 'Give me one reason.'

'Well,' I said, 'This happened so fast, I was do-ing 35 miles an hour ...'

He said, 'The speed limit is 25 miles per hour.' Now he could arrest me for something he really hadn't stopped me for.

I said, 'I can't give you a reason, I'm just ask-ing for mercy.'

He let me go. He handed me back my driving licence and said, 'Go on!' I couldn't believe it! I didn't deserve it. But I thanked him. I have never forgotten how I felt.

There are several kinds of mercy in the Bible.

Saving mercy
This is what the apostle Paul had in mind when he wrote 1 Timothy 1:13: 'Even though I was once a blasphemer and a persecutor and a violent man, I was shown mercy.' And he said in verse 15: 'Here is a trustworthy saying that deserves full accept-ance: Christ Jesus came into the world to save sin-

ners – of whom I am the worst. But for that very reason I was shown mercy.' The Authorized Version says, 'I obtained mercy.'

Language like that, without the power of the Holy Spirit, will make no sense whatever. But when the Holy Spirit comes alongside, suddenly we are convicted of and ashamed of what we have done. We now see what John Newton wrote about in his well-known hymn 'Amazing Grace'. He saw that it was his own sins that put Jesus on the cross, and he felt so ashamed. All he could do was ask God for mercy.

The only way to be saved is to ask God for mercy. If you are not a Christian, ask God to save you because Jesus died for sinners. Good works will not save, joining a church will not save, being baptised will not save, turning over a new leaf will not save, giving money to the church will not save.

Sovereign mercy

Paul quotes God's words to Moses to describe this type of mercy:

> 'I will have mercy on whom I have mercy,
>   and I will have compassion on whom I have
>   compassion.'

It does not, therefore, depend on man's desire or effort, but on God's mercy' (Romans 9:15-16).

Sovereign mercy means that God, by his own will, withheld justice, but gave mercy.

When a person realizes that his destiny is in God's hands, and that God could save or condemn and still be just, the person should ask, 'How can he save me and still be just?' The answer is, 'Because his Son paid the debt on the cross by shedding his blood.' If that person tries to be saved any other way, he will be showing contempt for the blood of the Son of God.

Scandalous mercy

A judge would look bad for withholding justice from a particular kind of criminal. But mercy is given by God to those who are so undeserving that it makes God look bad for saving them. But Hosea saw this in advance: 'I will call them "my people" who are not my people; and I will call her "my lovely one" who is not my loved one' (Romans 9:25). This is the way it is put in 1 Peter 2:8: human beings found this gospel offensive, and stumbled because they disobeyed the message of sheer grace. The Greek word describing the offence is *skandalon*, from which we get the word 'scandalous'. But God loves the most difficult case imaginable. There's nothing that brings him greater honour than showing mercy to the greatest sinner.

John Newton requested that his tombstone in Olney be inscribed with these words: 'A clerk, once an infidel and libertine, a servant of slaves in Africa, was by the rich mercy of our Lord and Saviour Jesus Christ preserved, restored, pardoned and appointed to preach the faith he had long laboured to destroy.'

He was a man who stooped to the level of a servant of slaves in Africa. He had lost all sense of dignity. His immorality was so horrible that biographers are ashamed to say what he was like. But God saved him and made him a trophy of grace.

If you are prepared to say, 'I know there is one hope of my being saved, and that is Jesus died for me,' that's asking God for mercy.

Sought mercy

This is the type of mercy that is described in Psalm 123. The psalmist was seeking for mercy from God, and was determined to keep looking to him until he found it. This is what every Christian prays for: 'Let us then approach the throne of grace with confidence, so that we may receive mercy' (Hebrews 4:16). Christians never outgrow asking for mercy.

Dear fellow-Christian, maybe this is one of the reasons you haven't had your prayers answered. Have you been guilty of rushing into the presence of God, snapping your fingers, and asking God to do this and that? Some Christians have the idea that God is nothing more than a heavenly Father

Christmas, there to give presents when asked.

But the God of the Bible is the same God who said to Moses, 'I will have mercy on whom I will have mercy, and will be gracious to whom I will be gracious.' That should bring us to our knees as we realize we have no bargaining power with God. All we can do is look to him and say, 'I am not leaving! I am not giving up! I have got nowhere else to go!'

The way we are saved, in the words of Luke 18:13, is by saying, 'God, have mercy on me, a sinner.' The way we are kept after conversion is by the same mercy of God. It is true that once we are made members of the family, God will never cast us out: 'Surely goodness and mercy shall follow me all the days of my life' (Psalm 23:6, *AV*).

5

Psalm 124

The great escape

If the LORD had not been on our side —
    let Israel say —
if the LORD had not been on our side
    when men attacked us,
when their anger flared against us,
    they would have swallowed us alive;
the flood would have engulfed us,
    the torrent would have swept over us,
the raging waters
    would have swept us away.
Praise be to the LORD,
    who has not let us be torn by their teeth.
We have escaped like a bird
    out of the fowler's snare;
the snare has been broken,
    and we have escaped.
Our help is in the name of the LORD,
    the Maker of heaven and earth.

As we looked at the other psalms in the series, I pointed out what I believe to be the operative word, the word that often summarizes the meaning of each particular psalm. The word in Psalm 124 is *escaped*. It is used twice, in verses 7 and 8:

> We have *escaped* like a bird
> out of the fowler's snare;
> The snare has been broken
> and we have *escaped*.

This psalm was sung as the pilgrims reflected over God's mercy.

I wonder whether Psalm 124 has been particularly special to you? Or maybe, although the words of this psalm didn't come to mind at the time, still you know there was an instance when you were spared or rescued just in the nick of time. You can see how easily things might have gone differently, causing your whole life to change course. You know what it is like for the Lord to rescue you. Maybe you didn't see God in it at the time, but that is the only real explanation. God mercifully stepped in.

In this psalm, God's people were the objects of attack: 'If the LORD had not been on our side when men attacked us ...' Do you know what it is like to have somebody attack you physically? The trauma is one that humanly speaking you don't get over. Or perhaps you have been attacked verbally. You

know the awful feeling when somebody points the
finger at you in blame.

But let me tell you who your real enemy is. It is
the devil. The devil's work is to cloud your mind.
He can come as an angel of light; that means that
he will work through someone who has the appearance of being very righteous, a person of in-
tegrity, a person who is believable. Or he may come
as a roaring lion. Do you know what it is to be on
the side of righteousness and have the devil attack
you?

The Lord's people in this psalm were the objects of anger. It is very frightening to be near
someone who is angry. Perhaps you are constantly
in fear of the temper of someone you work with,
or perhaps you are perpetually afraid of the anger
of someone you live with. You know how it feels
to live in a situation from which you wish you could
be delivered. But we learn from verse 6 that God
can step in to the situation: 'Praise be to the LORD
who has not let us be torn by their teeth.'

The psalmist said, 'We have escaped like a bird
out of the fowler's snare.' There are five examples
of snares that I want to point out in this chapter. It
could be that right now you are in the devil's grip,
unaware of what is happening. But I want you to
see that it is the devil.

Out of the fowler's snare

The first snare is *bad company*. Paul wrote in 1 Corinthians 15:33: 'Do not be misled: bad company corrupts good character.' And in 2 Corinthians 6:14, he wrote:

Do not be yoked together with unbelievers. For what do righteousness and wickedness have in common? Or what fellowship can light have with darkness? What harmony is there between Christ and Belial? What does a believer have in common with an unbeliever? What agreement is there between the temple of God and idols? For we are the temple of the living God. As God has said: 'I will live with them and walk among them, and I will be their God, and they will be my people.'

'Therefore come out from them
and be separate,'

says the Lord.

'Touch no unclean thing,
and I will receive you.'

'I will be a Father to you,
and you will be my sons and daughters,
says the Lord Almighty.'

Could it be that at this moment you are in this snare? You are trapped with bad company, and they

are doing you no good. Maybe, however, you have
rationalized the situation and made up excuses,
concluding that you can be an exception. You
wouldn't recommend anybody else to do what you
are doing.

The worst thing that you can do, however, is to
begin to think that you are the exception to the
rule. For the devil will come alongside and say
that you are different, that you can associate with
wrong company. Then before you know it, you are
in a trap.

It is a wonderful thing to realize that God delivers us from bad company. Some years ago, I
was in a situation where I found myself unwittingly
in the grip of someone who I could see was not
good for me. The person was a professing Christian, but I found myself in his grip, and I was leaning on him. I realized that this was wrong and God
delivered me from the situation. I was so thankful.

Maybe you are in a situation where you are being wrongly influenced, and as a consequence have
lost the sense of inner peace. Where the Spirit of the
Lord is, there is liberty. But bad company causes
you to lose the peace that God wants you to have.
I ask you, are you in the grip of bad company?

My second example of a snare is *uncontrolled
ambition*. Now ambition is a good thing. Martin
Luther said that God uses sex to drive a man to
marriage, ambition to drive a man to service, and

fear to drive a man to faith. A person who has ambition and is highly motivated can be thankful because God gave that outlook. Yet it is possible to have an ambition that is out of control, and to do things primarily to win admiration from others.

I remember on one occasion being stopped in my tracks by Ecclesiastes 4:4: 'And I saw that all labour and all achievement spring from man's envy of his neighbour.' The writer of Ecclesiastes is saying that the reason things get done, the reason anything is accomplished, is because we are motivated by our desire for admiration or to make others envious.

You may say, 'I'm not like that,' and may think that you are the exception to the rule, that you don't focus on yourself in the slightest bit, that you don't care in the least what people think. Let me ask you a question: If you are in a group photo, whose picture do you look for first? Or let me put it to you another way. If you were invited to spend an evening with the Queen at Buckingham Palace, could you keep quiet about it?

Why is it we want to be seen with the right people? We want to get position.

There once was a popular book called *The Peter Principle*. The thesis of the book was that everyone is promoted to the level of his or her incompetence, the idea being that everybody has a job they shouldn't have. If they had stayed just one notch below, everything would have been all right. They wouldn't be making quite so much money, but they wouldn't have high blood pressure. Sometimes promotion comes because there is nobody else to do it, but often it comes because of ambition. A person is determined to get a particular job.

Sometimes the hardest thing in the world is to come to terms with what your gift really is, what your ability really is, and what it is that God wants for you. When I read Ecclesiastes 4:4, I couldn't think of anything else for three or four days. Why did I choose Oxford, and not just stay in the hills of Kentucky? I had to reassess whether it was God who had led me to where I was, or whether it was my ambition that was driving me. And I began to feel awful.

I prayed, 'Lord, is it possible that I could come to the place where all I want is your glory?' Jesus said, 'How can ye believe, which receive honour one of another, and seek not the honour that cometh from God only?' (John 5:44, AV). The greatest feeling in the world is when we come to the place where we know God knows that we want his honour.

It may be you are in the snare of uncontrolled ambition at the moment, determined to get some prestige, a little bit of honour. But God says, 'I want you to live just for my approval.'

The third snare is *overestimating your strength*. There is a good example of this type of snare in the Old Testament account of Abraham and Lot. These two men were related to each other; Lot was Abraham's nephew. When they went their separate ways, we are told in Genesis 13:12, that Lot 'pitched his tents near Sodom'. Sodom was renowned as a centre of wickedness and sinful pleasure, yet Lot chose to pitch his tent near there. If asked, he would say, 'I am strong enough.'

Some Christians imagine that strength is shown by how close they can get to the world without giving in to it. But this is not a sign of strength. The proof that one has strength is seen, not by how close one can get, but by knowing in advance what it will lead to and avoiding it.

When Lot began to live in that atmosphere, it was not long before his principles changed. Are you involved in something which in a previous time in your life you said would never happen to you? Perhaps you are compromising with finances. Perhaps you are going to places you know you shouldn't, and, if the truth were out, you would be in real trouble.

Sodom was a centre for homosexual practice. When the inhabitants saw two unusual people come to Lot's house, they wanted sexual relations with those two strangers, who, unknown to them, were angels. But the saddest part of the story is that Lot went out to meet the inhabitants and offered them his two virgin daughters. Can you imagine a father who would do a thing like that? Lot had stooped so low.

Do you know how it started? It started when Lot said, 'I am the exception to the rule. I am strong enough to live near Sodom.' His principles became so compromised that he was willing for his two daughters to be taken by those wicked men. See what happens when you overestimate your strength, and get too close to the world! Your principles are compromised.

However, that is not the end of that story. Lot mercifully was delivered. We are told, in 2 Peter 2:7, that Lot was a righteous man. This is rather strange when you think about it. But do you know why this could be said of him? He was a child of God, and a child of God is one who is regarded as righteous in God's sight, not on the basis of his own works but on the basis of what Jesus Christ did on the cross when he paid the penalty for sin.

The fourth snare is *temptation*. Paul wrote in Romans 13:14: 'Do not think about how to gratify the desires of the sinful nature.' If you know what will tempt you, but then go near it, you are asking for trouble. As I said earlier in the chapter, spiritual strength lies not in seeing how close you can get to temptation and still resist it, but in knowing that you are weak, and avoiding the temptation altogether. The best way to keep from falling into sin is to avoid temptation. The wonderful thing is that God provides a way of escape:

> No temptation has seized you except what is common to man. And God is faithful; he will not let you be tempted beyond what you can bear. But when you are tempted, he will also provide a way out so that you can stand up under it (1 Corinthians 10:13).

God will enable you to bear it, and he will rescue you.

The fifth example is the snare of *disobedience*. This occurs when God tells us what to do and we don't do it. It could be at this moment you are wrestling with something God has pinpointed in your life. It may be sin, it may be temptation, it may be a particular type of company. He may be telling you to go to a particular place, or to avoid a certain action. And at first glance, you may say, 'I can't do it! I'm not up to it!' But God is serious about what he wants you to do.

Jonah ran from God. When he was praying in the belly of the fish, God gave him a second chance. God has a way of bringing you to the point where you begin to pray for a second chance to do what, at one time, you didn't want to do. God didn't have to come to Jonah the second time, but he did. Jonah was so glad to have another opportunity.

Our help is in the name of the LORD

No matter how greatly you have suffered, how
deeply involved you are with bad company, where
your ambition has led you, or how many times you
have disobeyed God, he is able to rescue you if
you call on his name.

At the beginning of Psalm 124 David said, 'If
the LORD had not been on our side ...' But you may
be saying, 'I don't think God *is* on my side.' Remember this, God is on the side of anybody who
will openly identify with his son, Jesus Christ. God
has promised that everything that happens in the
lives of believers will work together for their good.

6

Psalm 125

Eternal security

Those who trust in the LORD are like Mount Zion,
  which cannot be shaken but endures for ever.
As the mountains surround Jerusalem,
  so the LORD surrounds his people
  both now and for evermore.
The sceptre of the wicked will not remain
  over the land allotted to the righteous,
for then the righteous might use
  their hands to do evil.
Do good, O LORD, to those who are good,
  to those who are upright in heart.
But those who turn to crooked ways
  the LORD will banish with the evildoers.
Peace be upon Israel.

Psalm 125 describes our eternal security as Christians. I was brought up to believe the opposite of what I am now going to say on this subject.

All Christians believe the important doctrines of the faith, such as the deity of Jesus, his dying for us on the cross for our sins, his resurrection from the dead, and that he is the only way to get to heaven.

But it can be different when it comes to what I call the subheadings of Christian doctrine. With regard to eternal security, there are those who believe that once a person is saved, if he or she does not walk the straight and narrow way, and were to die in that condition, he or she would go to hell as though he or she had never been saved.

A number of years ago I had an unusual experience of the Holy Spirit. What happened was this: for a few seconds I was given an assurance of salvation that went so deep I could never express in words what it was like. I knew beyond any doubt that not only was I saved, but that I was saved for ever.

I had been taught the opposite, however, and I had to come to terms with the fact that this was one area where I had been taught wrongly. I had to make a change. Maybe you have had to make a change. Perhaps you had an opinion on something that you held dearly, but then something happened and you had to change your mind. Maybe you still need to change your mind.

The truth of eternal security is this: once a person confesses his sins to God, and trusts in Jesus, who died as an atonement on the cross, he is converted. The person who has done that is saved for ever, even if he or she doesn't know it. It is possible for a person to be converted and still not believe in eternal security.

This is a great pity, because it is good to know that, whatever else is true, I am going to be in heaven. What happened to me with that experience of the Holy Spirit was just this, I knew I was going to heaven. It was as though I was already there. I was given a little bit of heaven to go to heaven on.

Look at Psalm 125:1-2:

Those who trust in the LORD are like
    Mount Zion,
  which cannot be shaken but endures
    for ever.
As the mountains surround Jerusalem,
  so the LORD surrounds his people
  both now and for evermore.

That is the psalmist's doctrine of eternal security.

There are people who are saved but who, because of what they have done since becoming a

Christian, have come to doubt that it was real. They have concluded that no Christian could live like that, so either they have lost their salvation or had never been saved in the first place.

The last thing I want to do is to give false assurance. But if at any time in your past, through the convicting power of the Holy Spirit, you came to realize that you were lost and you received Jesus into your heart as your Lord and Saviour, then you have been converted.

God hasn't forgotten you. What he wants you to do is to get things right again. He will use you, though your life has been in a mess, if you are sorry for the way you have lived. Why do you suppose you are sorry? It is because you are a child of God.

Psalm 125 as a whole describes two kinds of people, the only two kinds of people in the whole world: those who have trusted in the true God, and those who haven't. Verses 1 and 2 describe the first category and verses 3 and 4 describe the second category.

There are three things about those who do put their trust in the Lord that I want to highlight.

They are selected

Mount Zion is another name for Jerusalem, which, as we saw in Psalm 122, was a chosen city. Paul tells us in Ephesians 1:4 that every person who is saved was chosen by God. Writing to Timothy, Paul also said:

> So do not be ashamed to testify about our Lord, or ashamed of me his prisoner. But join with me in suffering for the gospel, by the power of God, who has saved us and called us to a holy life – not because of anything we have done but because of his own purpose and grace. This grace was given us in Christ Jesus before the beginning of time (2 Timothy 1:8, 9).

It is possible that the only sense of security you have is that the Lord has chosen you, that he has set his affection on you. It could be that when it comes to getting a job, you have been rejected; when it comes to finding a friend, you have been rejected. Perhaps you have been rejected by a parent or by a schoolteacher. Perhaps you have not been selected for anything in this world. But what does it matter if you have come to trust in Jesus.

They are surrounded

Not only are all those who trust in the Lord selected, they are also surrounded. Notice how this is put in verse 2: 'As the mountains surround Jerusalem, so the LORD surrounds his people both now and for evermore.' So far, in all these psalms, I have suggested that one operative word gives a kind of a key to each psalm. In this psalm the word is *surrounds*.

How does the Lord surround his people? One way he does it is by *angels*. Angels are God's messengers, sent to serve those who will inherit salvation (Hebrews 1:14). Psalm 34:7 says, 'The angel of the LORD encamps around those who fear him, and he delivers them.' As surely as you have trusted in the Lord, you have at least one angel with you at all times. No question about it.

Of course, the angels remain invisible. We are unable to see them because of the danger that we would start talking to them instead of the Lord. When the apostle John was on the isle of Patmos, godly and knowledgeable and mature though he was, he wrongly fell down to worship an angel (Revelation 22:8). That amazes me. The reason we cannot see angels is that we would worship them.

Believers are also surrounded by *affection*. David sang in Psalm 139:17-18: 'How precious to me are your thoughts, O God! How vast is the sum of them! Were I to count them, they would outnumber the grains of sand.' Have you ever picked up a handful of sand and tried to guess how many grains you were holding? There is one thing I am convinced of: when we get to heaven and find out just how much God loves us, we will feel ashamed that we could ever have doubted his love.

But not only are believers surrounded by angels and by God's affection, they are also surrounded by *admonitions*. Listen to this word from
Psalm 19:11: 'By them is your servant warned.'
What does he mean by *them*? He is referring to
the commandments of the Lord.

Although we are loved with an everlasting love,
God doesn't like it when we step out of line. Eternal security is not a blank cheque to live as we
please. If we start doing so, God will chasten us
severely. We should never cast our eyes in the direction of the world, the flesh and the devil, to what
is sinful, to anything that is unlike Jesus. God does
not save us in order to give us a green light to live
any way we please. If we do disobey him, he has a
way of putting us flat on our backs to make us
listen to him, and say, 'God, I'm sorry!'

It is because we are saved that God deals with
us like that. He entered into a covenant with us.
He owns us; we are bought with a price.

All believers are surrounded by warnings. God
is saying to each of them, 'Don't be a fool.'

They are secure

Not only are those who trust in the Lord *selected*
and *surrounded*, they are *secure*. How secure? Let
me put it like this. God loves them as much as the
Father loves Jesus. In John 17:23, Jesus actually
prayed, 'May they be brought to complete unity to

let the world know that you sent me and have loved them even as you have loved me.' And Romans 8:17 says that all who are saved are 'joint-heirs with Jesus'.

Have you any idea how much God loves Jesus? God loves his Son far more than we as parents love our children. What chance do you think that Jesus has of being dislodged from the Trinity? Do you think there is any possibility that Jesus could somehow be disenfranchised, and the Father say, 'I don't want you any more!'? No, it is not possible. And those who trust in the Lord are secure for evermore. They are surrounded by love and cannot be dislodged. Who shall separate them from the love of Christ? Who will bring any charge against those whom God has chosen? They are loved with an everlasting love.

Those who trust in the Lord have had the righteousness of Jesus transferred to them. This transaction is called *imputed righteousness*. It means that God puts to their credit the very righteousness of Jesus as though they were that righteousness. That is why they are secure.

Those who are in Christ are selected, surrounded and secure.

7

Psalm 126

When the nightmare is over

When the Lord brought back the captives to Zion,
　　we were like men who dreamed.
Our mouths were filled with laughter,
　　our tongues with songs of joy.
Then it was said among the nations,
　　'The Lord has done great things for them.'
The Lord has done great things for us,
　　and we are filled with joy.
Restore our fortunes, O Lord,
　　like streams in the Negev.
Those who sow in tears
　　will reap with songs of joy.
He who goes out weeping,
　　carrying seed to sow,
will return with songs of joy,
　　carrying sheaves with him.

For years I have been gripped b
verses 5 and 6 of this psalm:

> Those who sow in tears
>> will reap with songs of joy.
> He who goes out weeping,
>> carrying seed to sow,
> will return with songs of joy,
>> carrying sheaves with him.

Here is a promise that is based on a condition. The promise is joy, even success, but the condition is tears.

Has something ever broken your heart? Have you ever felt that because your heart is breaking, all you can do is weep? Some people can cry at the drop of a hat, but I'm not referring to that kind of tears. Some men are afraid to cry, they feel that it is not manly. But the greatest man that ever was, Jesus of Nazareth, wept (John 11:35).

Psalm 126 refers to the end of a nightmare: 'When the LORD brought back the captives to Zion, we were like men who dreamed.' In other words, it seemed too good to be true. But while the nightmare was on, they thought it would never end.

A nightmare is an awful thing. I think that some of them may be caused by the devil. The last thing I do before I fall asleep is to pray for the sprinkling of the blood of Jesus upon my family and myself. I pray so every night, because I know the devil likes to seize upon us in our sleep, when we cannot control what is happening.

The nightmare referred to in Psalm 126 was that of Israel living in captivity in Babylon, a captivity that lasted for seventy years. Many died there and others were born there. The whole time they lived in Babylon, all they could think about was going home.

Maybe you have experienced the opposite of a nightmare, when what is actually happening just seems too good to be true? In the previous chapter I referred to the greatest spiritual experience I have had so far; I was given assurance from the Lord that I was eternally saved. I often wish something like that would happen again. I was going around like one who dreamed.

Many Americans will know the statement made by Gerald Ford when he was inaugurated as President: 'Our long national nightmare is over.' He had become President following the disgraceful fall of President Nixon, and those words gave comfort to Americans at the time. They were healing words. In this chapter I would like to give healing words.

You may be enduring a psychological or emotional nightmare, where you think you are losing your mind because the depression is so severe and the anxiety so intense.

Maybe you are facing a financial nightmare,

being deep in debt. I think of those in our society who are elderly and have to survive on small incomes. It is very sad to think of them being put under that kind of pressure.

Perhaps it is a physical nightmare that you face, where something has gone wrong inside your body and the outlook is bleak.

Perhaps you are going through a social nightmare. You have been ostracized because of the colour of your skin or because of your accent.

Sometimes the nightmare is God's severe chastening. It is enforced learning. The Bible puts it like this: 'Whom the Lord loves, he chastens' (Hebrews 12:6). It means God is on your case, and is forcing you to notice him. You say, 'Well, why would he do that?' Because he loves you. He may put you through a particular kind of ordeal that hurts a lot, and you think, 'Why the continuing storm?' I'll tell you why – you haven't learned yet.

There is also what I call pre-conversion disciplining. God may bring certain people into a nightmare in broad daylight, because he is on their case. If you are in a pre-conversion nightmare, I'm glad about that! For when it is over, you will be able to say, 'I can't believe God loves me so much that he would go to such great pains to get my attention.'

The nightmare may be punishment. Israel had been punished because they had forgotten God. They were God's chosen people. I don't know why

God chose Israel, but he did. And you can't deny it; the Bible makes it clear. God said to Abraham, 'I will bless those who bless you and I will curse those who curse you' (Genesis 12:3). Jews felt comfortable with that. They knew that God had chosen Jerusalem. They assumed that God would never punish them. Maybe you're like that! Don't be a fool!

The prophet, Jeremiah, stood alone and said, 'It will happen to you!' Some false prophets said that it would not happen. But Jeremiah was right. The armies of Babylon came into the city, burned down the temple, and took the most qualified of the people back to Babylon. Only the very poor were left behind.

I am not saying that the nightmare you may be experiencing is God getting even with you. I do know, however, that it was in a sense that way with Israel. But let me put it this way. According to 1 Peter 2:20, there are two kinds of punishment. There is the suffering that comes because one did what was wrong and there is suffering for doing good. 'It is better, if it is God's will, to suffer for doing good than for doing evil' (1 Peter 3:17). So it is possible that your nightmare could be God punishing you. It is equally possible that the nightmare is because you are obedient and it is God's way of making you more like Jesus. 'For it is commendable if a man bears up under the pain of unjust suffering because he is conscious of God' (1 Peter 2:19).

But the nightmare will end. God knows how much we can bear, and even when he chastens in the sense of punishment, he knows how much each of us can take.

When the nightmare is over, it could mean a *restoration of honour*. In verse 4 the psalmist said, 'Restore our fortunes, O LORD.' It could be that your good name is under a cloud. Maybe you have done something that has caused people to raise their eyebrows, or perhaps you have been falsely accused and you long to have your name cleared.

It could be a *restoration of holiness*. Are you a backslider? Have you been living in sin and just doing anything that your body feels like? It is not worth it.

It could be a *restoration of humility*: 'Those who sow in tears, will reap with songs of joy' (verse 6). Perhaps you have become proud and unmanageable and God has had to humble you.

The first time the word 'tears' appears in the Bible is in 2 Kings 20:5. Hezekiah had been told his time was up: 'You will die, you will not recover' (verse 1). Hezekiah pleaded with the Lord to reverse the decision. Isaiah gave him the good word; Hezekiah would not die then after all: 'I have heard your prayer and seen your tears'.

Try tears. They get God's attention. They also

get the attention of the lost. My old friend Ernest Reisinger tells what led to his conversion, seeing the tears in the eyes of the man who had been patiently witnessing to him.

Hannah wept because she was barren. God gave her Samuel. The church whose womb has been strategically closed by God may find the answer in sowing in tears, that God could say 'Sing, O barren woman, you who never bore a child ... For a brief moment I abandoned you, but with deep compassion I will bring you back' (Isaiah 54:1,7).

'Weeping may remain for a night, but rejoicing comes in the morning' (Psalm 30:5).

Do you want to know the way back? It is the way of tears, sorrow that is true repentance. When you are sorry, the way to end the nightmare is to weep. God sees tears.

8

Psalm 127

When God says 'Yes'

Unless the LORD builds the house,
   its builders labour in vain.
Unless the LORD watches over the city,
   the watchmen stand guard in vain.
In vain you rise early
   and stay up late,
toiling for food to eat –
   for he grants sleep to those he loves.
Sons are a heritage from the LORD,
   children a reward from him.
Like arrows in the hands of a warrior
   are sons born in one's youth.
Blessed is the man
   whose quiver is full of them.
They will not be put to shame
   when they contend with their enemies in the
                                        gate.

I don't know what we are going to do when we get to heaven. One thing I am sure of, however, is that we will get to see what it would have been like to have been with those pilgrims on their way to Jerusalem. We will discover the meaning of details we can but speculate on. But one thing which needs no speculation is verse 1 of Psalm 127:

> Unless the LORD builds the house,
>   its builders labour in vain.
> Unless the LORD watches over the city,
>   the watchmen stand guard in vain.

The heading of the psalm is 'A song of ascents. Of Solomon.' C. H. Spurgeon wasn't sure whether David wrote this for his son, Solomon, or whether Solomon himself wrote it. But either way it is a reference to the temple.

David had an ambition that he did not get to see fulfilled. Do you know what it is like to want something more than anything in the world, and for God to say, 'No. That's one thing you can't have'? David had conquered Jerusalem and become king of Israel. But when he indicated his desire to build a temple for the Lord, God would not let him. David had to come to terms with the situation. He couldn't do what he wanted. So it may have been David who wrote these words: 'Unless the LORD builds the house, its builders labour in vain.'

I wonder if you are like that. God has been good to you and you have accomplished much. Many things have happened to you; you have gone far, and people are envious of you. 'What more could that person want?' they ask. But you do want more, and for a while you had a hope that you would get what you wanted. But then God said, 'No'.

I was named after my father's favourite preacher, Dr R. T. Williams. He was known by his initials, R. T., and I have never known anything in my life but 'R.T.' R. T. Williams said, 'Within God's will there is no failure. Outside God's will there is no success.' That is another way of saying that unless the Lord builds the house, the builders will labour in vain.

What if David had gone ahead and built the temple? Maybe you have been stopped from do-ing something that you wanted to do. But you are the type who has always managed to get your way. So even though God says, 'No', you say, 'Don't tell me I can't do it!'

Unless the Lord ...

In this chapter I want to focus on two things. The first is when God says 'No', and the second is when God says 'Yes'. In this psalm we have both his 'No' and his 'Yes'.

When God says 'No', the wisest thing to do is to take him seriously. If God says 'No', but you say, 'I am going to do it anyway', then you are a fool. Has God said 'No' to you about anything? Has he put his finger on something in your life? Let me tell you what God says 'No' to. He says 'No' to sexual promiscuity; he says 'No' to drugs and the abuse of your body; he says 'No' to drunkenness; he says 'No' to telling lies. God says 'No' and he means it. Bitterness. Holding a grudge. Vindicating yourself. Complaining.

But you know, it is surprising what God says 'No' to, sometimes even to things one would have thought he would surely say 'Yes' to. In Acts 16:6, we read that 'Paul and his companions travelled throughout the region of Phrygia and Galatia, having been kept by the Holy Spirit from preaching the word in the province of Asia.' Isn't it interesting that God said 'No' to preaching the word in Asia. We would have thought that when it comes to preaching the word, God would surely say 'Yes', but God said 'No'. In fact, the next verse says that when they came to a certain place and tried to enter, the Holy Spirit said 'No'. This shows that God even determines where the gospel is preached, and who gets to hear it.

There are two kinds of God's 'No'. One is a warning. Psalm 19:10-11 says of God's warnings:

They are more precious than gold,
than much pure gold;

they are sweeter than honey,
    than honey from the comb.
By them is your servant warned;
    in keeping them there is great reward.

But the other kind of 'No' is when God makes
it plain that you had better stop trying to do what
he isn't in. One way God works is to take his hand
off and just leave it to you. Then if you try to do it
in your own strength, you will see the folly of it.
Sometimes, however, he will actually work against
you. The people of Israel discovered this (Numbers 14:40-45).

There are some great enemies in the world, but
there is one enemy we don't want. There is somebody
we don't want working against us, and that's
God. I don't want him angry with me.

God knows that when he says 'No', it is always
right. It is only a matter of time before you will be
thankful for the closed door.

One of the greatest disappointments of my life
was not being called by a church in Florida that I
had thought *was* going to call me to be their minister.
But I have lived to be so thankful. I eventually
saw the wisdom of God. Maybe you are coming
up against a closed door that you are trying to
pry open. Unless the Lord opens the door, you are
a fool to pry it open.

Implied in this psalm is also the positive side,

when God says 'Yes'. What does that mean? It is when we set our hearts to do something, and it just comes easily, because God is in it.

Somebody once asked me what I meant by the phrase 'wanting an anointing'. An anointing is what comes easily. When you have an anointing to do something, it comes with ease. I pray for it in ever increasing measure. But when you find fatigue and pressure, it means you have moved outside your anointing. When God puts you into a position, you will be able to do it.

I mentioned in an earlier chapter the best-selling book of some years ago, *The Peter Principle*, which put forward the theory that everyone is promoted to the level of his or her incompetence. We want a job because it pays more or brings with it a certain prestige. However, the truth is, having the job or position leads to high blood pressure and nervous twitches, wrinkles and sleepless nights. We may have the job, the prestige, the money, but we are heading for a nervous breakdown. It is far better to stay at a level where we can cope.

However, when God is in something, he grants us success and it comes easily.

I remember a period during our time in Fort Lauderdale, when it did not rain for several weeks and the grass in our front and back gardens turned yellow. We were in danger of losing the grass. Since we didn't have a water system, I had to take a hose and spend about six hours watering the grass. Finally, I finished. Guess what happened? Fifteen minutes later, there was a big black cloud, and it began to rain. It must have rained five inches! It did more good in forty-five minutes than I had done in six hours!

That is what it is like when God says 'Yes'. For when he says 'Yes', it makes a big difference. But to know this, we may have to fast and pray. If God is hiding his face from you, and you don't know what to do, go and spend a whole day in prayer and fasting.

What happens when God says 'Yes'
This psalm tells us what God does when he says 'Yes'.

First, he *builds* (verse 1). He supplies the energy and the materials. He supplies the labour and the success that had been so eluding. Things begin to happen. With ease. 'Throw your net on the right side of the boat,' said Jesus to frustrated disciples who fished all night without success, 'and you will find some' (John 21:6). They did: a total of 153 big fish! God said 'Yes'.

Secondly, God *watches* (verse 1). It is a wonderful thing to know God is looking after you. One of the most interesting accounts in the book of Ezra is where Ezra said that he was ashamed to ask the king for protection because he had already told

the king that God's hand was with Israel. But Ezra
knew he still needed God's help. And Ezra 8:23
says, 'So we fasted and petitioned our God about
this, and he answered our prayer.' If God says 'Yes',
we don't have to worry.

Thirdly, God *feeds* (verse 2). It is pointless to
wear yourself out toiling for food to eat, for if God
says 'Yes', he just supplies your need. Listen to
the words of Jesus in Matthew 6:25:

> Therefore I tell you, do not worry about your
> life, what you will eat or drink; or about your
> body, what you will wear. Is not life more im-
> portant than food, and the body more impor-
> tant than clothes? Look at the birds of the air;
> they do not sow or reap or store away in barns,
> and yet your heavenly Father feeds them. Are
> you not much more valuable than they?

My father's favourite verse was Matthew 6:33,
'But seek first his kingdom and his righteousness,
and all these things will be given to you as well.'

Fourthly, God grants *sleep* (verse 2). Sometimes
I have times of insomnia, everybody does at times.
It is worse if there is a hard day coming up. This
happened to me when we went to Hong Kong some
time ago. I thought I knew jet lag when I came
from America to Britain, but I had never experienced anything like what I felt after going from

Britain to Hong Kong. It was awful. I was to be on Hong Kong radio the next day. But I was awake all night.

This verse has since helped me to see that sleep comes from God, and if I don't get the sleep I think I need, it will still be OK. The radio interview went fairly well, and I made it through the day.

Within God's will there is no failure, outside God's will there is no success.

9

Psalm 128

The Health and Wealth gospel

Blessed are all who fear the LORD,
   who walk in his ways.
You will eat the fruit of your labour;
   blessings and prosperity will be yours.
Your wife will be like a fruitful vine
   within your house;
your sons will be like olive shoots
   round your table.
Thus is the man blessed
   who fears the LORD.
May the LORD bless you from Zion
   all the days of your life;
may you see the prosperity of Jerusalem,
   and may you live to see your children's children.
Peace be upon Israel.

My subject from this psalm is the Health and Wealth gospel, sometimes called 'Name it and claim it', or 'Believe it and receive it'. It is, in fact, what the apostle Paul would call 'another gospel'. It is not exactly what Paul was describing in Galatians 1:6-7, but his words are very appropriate: 'I am astonished that you are so quickly deserting the one who called you by the grace of Christ and are turning to a different gospel—which is really no gospel at all.'

The Health and Wealth gospel is not what the New Testament means by gospel. Instead its emphasis is not what happens to you when you die, but how well off you should be while you are still alive.

You may be one of those who say, 'That is what I want. I want something that will help me now. If I could just have my problems solved, then I would become a Christian.' I can understand that. There is no difficulty in seeing why so many people are attracted to the Health and Wealth gospel. There are many people with health worries or financial difficulties or marriage problems. I don't blame these people for wanting their difficulties solved.

What is this Health and Wealth gospel? The first thing it stresses is that it is God's will for you to be healed, no matter what is wrong with you. Secondly, it says that it is God's will for you to prosper financially. Therefore, if you are having any financial pressure, you are living beneath what God wants for you.

There are problems with this outlook, however. The first problem is that those who preach this false gospel tend to say that it is the devil who is keeping a person from either being healed or prospering. Therefore they say that the devil must be rebuked. There is something comfortable about being able to blame the devil, for it means never taking any personal responsibility.

Perhaps that is your problem. Maybe you want to blame your parents, your job, the person you have to work with, the government, even society. The whole world is to blame. The Health and Wealth gospel would enable you to blame the devil. Even if you have a headache, its adherents want to cast the devil out of you. But it's not biblical.

The other thing the advocates of the Health and Wealth gospel do is to blame a person's lack of faith if he or she is not healed or does not prosper. They don't have to explain their beliefs fully because they can just lay it on the person and create a guilt complex.

In effect, they can blame either the devil or the person for lack of faith.

There are those who keep on supporting preachers like that. I remember some years ago driving with a friend in Florida. We were listening to a radio broadcast by a particular speaker who was promising that God would take care of the financial problems of everyone who sent in ten dollars.

The Health and Wealth gospel, generally speaking, is preached by and supported by those who have virtually no concept of the sovereignty of God. Why do I say that? Because God is sovereign; for reasons of his own, without having to explain himself he can give or withhold blessing and be just either way. Sometimes he blesses and at other times he withholds blessing. The God of the Bible cannot be made to do things. He is God, and deserves our worship. This generation needs to come on bended knee to the God of the Bible who owes man nothing. Those who support the Health and Wealth gospel usually have no concept that God can give or withhold blessing and still be just.

Obviously I don't believe in the Health and Wealth gospel! But why refer to it?

One reason is because it is popular in America and it is coming to Britain. I wish it weren't so. There are a lot of imports from America about which we have to be very careful. We can understand why people would be interested in this 'gospel'. Yet the motivation comes from those who know they have nothing to lose by preaching it. They can live in their mansions and drive their flash cars, and say, 'God has blessed me.'

Another reason I am referring to it is because this psalm, if read superficially, could be taken to support the Health and Wealth gospel. Notice how it is put in verses 1 and 2:

Blessed are all who fear the LORD,
  who walk in his ways.
You will eat the fruit of your labour;
  blessings and prosperity will be yours.

Many Christians, when they read verses like that, think there is something wrong with them. Some of the godliest people that ever lived have stayed relatively poor and not known prosperity, and some have not known good health.

There are those who can't even find a wife (verse 3). I know others who have one and wish they didn't! I've known those in the ministry who have had the most unhappy marriages. Did you know that John Wesley was not happily married? His wife discouraged him and worked against him. It was a cross that he bore all his life. Did you know that George Whitefield was jilted and married a woman he didn't really love?

This psalm also says, 'your sons will be like olive shoots around your table' (verse 3). Yet there have been godly parents who, despite doing their best for their children, have lost them, and not found them following in the way of the Lord. No doubt, if the parents could relive their lives, they could think of things they would do differently.

The same is true in the Bible: Eli was a godly priest, but his sons went wrong; Samuel's sons were not equipped to follow him. It has often been like this.

How do we explain this in the light of this psalm?

Is there anything good about the Health and Wealth gospel?

I believe that there is. It shows what God *is able* to do in a day when people generally have no faith in God at all. We have to give the Health and Wealth people their dues: they have pointed out that there is a God in the heavens who answers prayer, and is willing to do far more for us than many of us have thought.

It stresses that God will do things today. There are those who are trapped into a closed, theological system, whereby they believe there is no possibility ever again of there being anything similar to what there was in the days of the apostles. But I have seen such things happen in my church, and we know they do occur elsewhere.

The Health and Wealth gospel stretches our faith with regard to things we might otherwise have not even thought about. There are those of us who say, 'I can't bother God with this problem. There are so many that have got worse problems than mine.' But if you start taking that line, then none of us would ever ask for anything. God has said,

'In all your ways acknowledge him, and he will make your paths straight' (Proverbs 3:6). It may be that he will heal a headache or a common cold or cancer. He may give you that job. He may solve the problem in your marriage. But we must bow down to his sovereignty in each case.

What is wrong with the Health and Wealth gospel?
First, it stresses only one side of the Scriptures. It is very selective and doesn't look at the Bible as a whole. Its advocates focus on verses such as 3 John 2, 'Dear friend, I pray that you may enjoy good health and that all may go well with you, even as your soul is getting along well', or Genesis 13:2 which states that Abraham had become very wealthy in livestock and in silver and gold.

They quote Isaiah 53:5:

> But he was pierced for our
>   transgressions,
>   he was crushed for our iniquities;
> the punishment that brought us peace
>   was upon him,
>   and by his wounds we are healed.

From this verse they argue that healing is in the atonement: 'Jesus died that you might be healed, and therefore you ought to be healed. If you are not healed, it's your fault!'

But that is only one half of the story. What about a verse like Philippians 4:12, where Paul states: 'I know what it is to be in need, and I know what it is to have plenty. I have learned the secret of being content in any and every situation, whether well fed or hungry, whether living in plenty or in want.'

Which takes greater faith? Is it faith to be healed? Is it faith to have money? Or is it faith to say to God, 'I worship you – even if I am in need'? That is faith, that is the proof of godliness. True Christianity does not promise that everything is going to be perfect.

Listen to other words of the apostle Paul, in 2 Corinthians 12:7-9, 'To keep me from becoming conceited because of these surpassingly great revelations, there was given me a thorn in my flesh, a messenger of Satan, to torment me. Three times I pleaded with the Lord to take it away from me. But he said to me, "My grace is sufficient for you, for my power is made perfect in weakness".'

We will never know until we get to heaven what Paul's thorn in the flesh was. Whatever it was, Paul prayed three times that it would leave him. What do the Health and Wealth gospel people say about that verse? I happen to know. My friend, O. S. Hawkins, was in Fort Worth, Texas, and he heard a Health and Wealth preacher say: 'If the apostle Paul had had my faith, he wouldn't have had his thorn in the flesh'. This just goes to show how low some will sink in order to justify what they believe.

Second, the Health and Wealth gospel has little to do with the reason God sent his Son into the world. This is why Paul would call the Health and Wealth gospel another gospel.

What is the true gospel? It is that God sent his Son into the world 2,000 years ago. Jesus of Nazareth was born of a virgin, and lived for thirty-three years on this earth. Then wicked men nailed him to a cross, but he was there as a substitute for sinners, bearing God's judgment on sin.

Maybe right at this moment you are preoccupied with your own problems. I understand that. But what will it matter one hundred years from now? Isn't God good to take into account the thing that really matters – what happens when we die? One can be blessed with healing and still go to hell. One can be blessed with prosperity and still be eternally lost.

What is wrong with the Health and Wealth emphasis? It stresses what God has to do, what he must do – which is monstrous – as opposed to what he may do. God doesn't *have* to do anything, he owes us nothing.

Let me point out that Psalm 128 is not a Psalm for the Health and Wealth gospel people after all. The psalmist finishes by saying, '*May* the LORD bless you from Zion all the days of your life; *may* you see the prosperity of Jerusalem, and *may* you live to see your children's children.' Why did he say that? Because God *may* not do it. We pray for it, but there is no certainty God will do it.

But what of the implications of this psalm? Is it not encouraging the very prosperity that some today promise? Am I not sweeping this psalm's purpose under the carpet?

I answer: this psalm, like the others, reflects the conditions of the Mosaic Covenant which promised prosperity if one was wholly obedient to the Law. 'If you fully obey the LORD your God and carefully follow all his commands ... all these blessings will come upon you and follow you' (Deuteronomy 28:1-2). Moses then promised the very kind of prosperity that this Psalm of Ascent contains (cf. Deuteronomy 28:2-14).

Jesus came to fulfil the Law (Matthew 5:17) – and did so (John 19:30). We therefore take our cue from Jesus who promised eternal life by faith in him and his death on the cross (John 3:16). He told us to seek first the Kingdom of God and his righteousness – not material things (Matthew 6:25-33).

We are only guaranteed that our needs will be given, a promise Paul also gave us (Philippians 4:19). Paul stated this after claiming 'I know what it is to be in need, and I know what it is to have plenty. I have learned the secret of being content in any and every situation, whether well fed or hungry, whether living in plenty or in want' (Philippians 4:12).

Then what is the relevance of this Psalm 128? That we may see that prosperity only comes from the Lord and that we will acknowledge our dependence upon him to give it. We do indeed pray for this. But it is not inevitable, otherwise the psalmist would not pray for it as he did. For, after all, whoever perfectly obeyed the Law in the first place?

10

Psalm 129

How to cope with the past

They have greatly oppressed me from my youth
   – let Israel say –
 they have greatly oppressed me from my youth,
    but they have not gained the victory over me.
Ploughmen have ploughed my back
   and made their furrows long.
But the LORD is righteous;
   he has cut me free from the cords of the wicked.
May all who hate Zion
   be turned back in shame.
May they be like grass on the roof,
   which withers before it can grow;
with it the reaper cannot fill his hands,
   nor the one who gathers fill his arms.
May those who pass by not say,
   'The blessing of the LORD be upon you;
   we bless you in the name of the LORD.'

It is not clear why this particular song was used. My own suggestion is this: God wanted Israel never to forget the pain their ancestors went through in order for them to have their heritage. Notice how the psalm begins:

They have greatly oppressed me from my youth
   – let Israel say –
they have greatly oppressed me from my youth,
    but they have not gained the victory over me.

God uses many ways to make sure his people don't forget what he has done for them. When Israel crossed the Jordan on their way to possess the land God had promised them, they erected twelve stones as a memorial for future generations (Joshua 4:20-23). The Lord's Supper is a remembrance of what Jesus did on the cross for us.

Psalm 129, however, refers primarily to the way Israel had suffered since its beginnings, which can be traced to Egypt. We can read the story in the Book of Exodus. The Israelites had become slaves in Egypt where they were forced to work in grim conditions until they were delivered by Moses. Hundreds of years later the psalmist composed this psalm lest these events be forgotten.

What could it be that God wants you to remember? It could be things you take for granted.

This was the way God dealt with King David.

God said to him, 'I took you from the pasture and from following the flock to be ruler over my people Israel' (2 Samuel 7:8). Why did God say that to David? Although David was Israel's greatest king, God would not let him forget the pit from which he was dug.

There are some Christians who, after they have enjoyed a little bit of success, become arrogant, conceited, sophisticated and pretentious; such do not want others to know what they were like in the past. It would have been easy for David to be like that, so God had a way of keeping him humble.

Maybe you know what it is like to have a similar kind of background, but you don't want anybody to know it. Are you ashamed of your background? The worst thing that can happen to a person is to become pretentious, to act as if he or she was somebody else.

For when it comes to our past, God knows everything. God wants to bring us to the place where we can be ourselves. We do not have to pretend, because God knows us. We also know that he has forgiven us.

Sometimes, however, the way to cope with the past is to forget it. Paul wrote in Philippians 3:13: 'But one thing I do: Forgetting what is behind...' What is certain is that we must not let past failure nor our lack of spiritual progress immobilize us.

This psalm is written for anybody who knows

what it is to have been oppressed in the past. There are three things I want us to learn from this psalm.

Firstly, this psalm is a reminder that the Christian belongs to a new family, a family with a past. Its history includes what the Bible says about Israel. The past for the family is riddled with persecution and hate.

Never think that the church will somehow gain the respect of everybody, or that, because you became a Christian, people are going to congratulate you. Those in the family will welcome you and be genuinely thrilled that you are a part of it, but outside the family you are not going to be respected. They may think you have a nervous condition or are in a state of emotional distress, but they will never think you have done something sensible.

Jesus never tried to make converts by offering an easy life. Instead, he said this: 'If anyone would come after me, he must deny himself and take up his cross daily and follow me. For whoever wants to save his life will lose it, but whoever loses his life for me will save it' (Luke 9:23-24). That is not what you would expect Jesus to say if he was trying to win a lot of converts. Jesus put it like this: 'They will put you out of the synagogue; in fact, a time is coming when anyone who kills you will think he is offering a service to God' (John 16:2).

This psalm is a reminder that the Christian joins

a family with a past wracked by persecution.

Well, if that's the case, why become a Christian? Because you will find forgiveness for all of your sins. Every sinful thing you have ever done will be washed away. There is only one way to know forgiveness of sins, and that is to confess that you have sinned against God. The only way your sins are forgiven is by the blood Jesus shed on the cross of Calvary.

Secondly, we have in this psalm a reminder that the gates of hell will never prevail against the church: 'They have greatly oppressed me from my youth, but they have not gained the victory.' God preserved the people of Israel in the Old Testament and the church since New Testament times.

One of the greatest proofs of the truth of the Bible is the Jewish race. How they have been preserved! People have always hated the Jews because of God's special love to them. Similarly, down the centuries, Christians have faced persecution. Yet that has never worked to extinguish anybody whose hand God was on. One of the early church fathers, Tertullian, coined a phrase: 'The blood of the martyrs is the seed of the church.' The more persecution there was, the more the church grew. The martyrdoms of Cranmer, Latimer, Ridley and others during the reign of Mary Tudor (1553-1558), instead of wiping out the faith, only ensured that believers would multiply all the more.

Thirdly, this psalm is a reminder that some have a past full of hurts. Perhaps that describes you. If that is the case, remember two things: in the Christian family there will be fellow believers who have suffered in a way similar to you, who can sympathize with you; best of all, Jesus will sympathize with you.

What is oppression? It is cruelty or pressure from outside that has been thrust upon you, in contrast to depression which comes from within. There are some people who have such a keen sense of rejection, that they just can't handle a situation where someone tries to love them. They believe somehow it won't be true.

But even though you have been oppressed and have known rejection and hurt or have damaged emotions, these experiences will not save you. You may think that because of these experiences you deserve a special break and somehow God will let you into heaven. But he will not.

A lot of people, if they have had some kind of hurt, have not got the victory over their attitude towards the problem. Instead they let the situation have the victory over them. It is possible for such people to allow their experiences to ruin them, instead of letting God use them to help others who are going through the same thing.

Let me tell you how to cope with your past. It is not to say, 'This is the way I am', it is to say with the psalmist, 'But they have not gained the victory.'

It could well be that you have known some deep hurt, that somebody has taken advantage of you.

It could be that you have what a psychologist would call arrested development. The idea is that too little or too much gratification at a certain age brings about an arrested emotional development. For example, did you ever see a person who was thirty years old, but had the emotions of a five year old? They may have an advanced intellect, but have the emotional standing of a child. They make poor marriage partners because they want a husband or wife to treat them the way they were as they grew up. But God can take a spoiled person and change him or her in a way that he can use.

Listen to these words from Lamentations 3:19-21:

'I remember my affliction and my wandering, the bitterness and the gall. I well remember them, and my soul is downcast within me. Yet, this I call to mind and therefore I have hope. Because of the LORD's great love we are not consumed.'

And then the writer says in verse 27: 'It is good for a man to bear the yoke while he is young.' It could be that while you were young, you knew severe suffering. You *can* make it good if you will affirm God.

What about the last part of this psalm? The psalmist says:

> May all who hate Zion
>   be turned back in shame.
> May they be like grass on the housetops,
>   which withers before it can grow;
> with it the reaper cannot fill his hands,
>   nor the one who gathers fill his arms.
> May those who pass by not say,
>   'The blessing of the LORD be upon you;
>   we bless you in the name of the LORD.'

Maybe you have spent your life wanting vengeance upon society, or upon a particular person. You may think this psalm is encouraging such an attitude.

But note, this psalm refers to *those* who hated Zion, not an individual. When it comes to the honour of God's name, then we pray that *all* who hate the church will be dealt with; it is not a personal issue. When we do experience a personal hurt, then we don't have the right to say those words. We must deal with the anger towards those who caused the hurt or towards God for allowing it. We must deal with the bitterness. If we do, God grants us a sweetness of spirit which will lead us actually to pray for those who caused the hurt.

You can be one of those exceedingly rare people who can say, 'But they did not get the victory.'

11

Psalm 130

When God is on your case

Out of the depths I cry to you, O LORD;
   O Lord, hear my voice.
Let your ears be attentive
   to my cry for mercy.

If you, O LORD, kept a record of sins,
   O Lord, who could stand?
But with you there is forgiveness;
   therefore you are feared.

I wait for the LORD, my soul waits,
   and in his word I put my hope.
My soul waits for the Lord
   more than watchmen wait for the morning,
   more than watchmen wait for the morning.

O Israel, put your hope in the LORD,
   for with the LORD is unfailing love
   and with him is full redemption.
He himself will redeem Israel
   from all their sins.

The title for this chapter, *When God is on your case*, is an expression I have been using for about two years. A friend of both Louise and me, who has a ministry of intercessory prayer, came into our lives a year or two ago. He claimed that God had laid me on his heart. When he came to talk with me, he would start weeping. He would say to me, 'R.T., God is on your case.' I had never heard the expression, but I felt that I knew what it meant.

Is God on your case? When this happens, it has to be the most wonderful thing in all the world. It means at least two things. The first is that God loves you, and the second is that he has special plans for you.

Let me use Job as an example. When we first meet Job, he has seven sons and three daughters; he owns 7,000 sheep, 3,000 camels, 500 yoke of oxen and 500 donkeys; he has a large number of servants. He was the greatest man among all the people of the east. When the story closes, we find that Job had twice as much. Yet we know the terrible troubles that happened to Job in between to cause this great increase of blessing.

I am not hinting that if God is on your case he is going to double your finances or increase your prosperity. I don't believe that. But what I am saying is this: if he has special plans for you, because he has set his affection on you, then he begins to deal with you. He gives you a new way of looking at things. Psalm 130 is about such a situation. It shows us seven ways that we can know if God is on our case.

The first way we know God is on our case is that he *gets our attention*. Look at verse 1.

> Out of the depths I cry to you, O LORD;
>   O Lord, hear my voice.
> Let your ears be attentive
>   to my cry for mercy.

How does God get our attention? He does it by bringing us into the depths. He brings us to the place where the only way we can look is *up*.

Can you recall a time when you looked down on everybody? Maybe you were on top of the world and were the envy of all who knew you. Then something happened, the situation was reversed and you began to lose things that you had taken for granted. Now your reputation isn't what it was; your financial security is not what it was; your health is not what it was. You have been brought to such a low ebb that you are in despair and cannot see any way forward. The only way you can look is up. I am saying that God is behind all this in order to get your attention.

The second way we know God is on our case is when we begin to pray *with tears*: 'Out of the depths I *cry* to you.'

The reason why you haven't been heard by God

is possibly because you have not cried. But you say, 'Surely God hears everything that is said.' In a sense that's true, but for reasons that I don't fully understand, tears make a difference with God. Do you have a hard heart that is so cold? Maybe you have even laughed at people who weep, seeing it as a sign of weakness. What you need is *broken-ness*. As David said in Psalm 51:17: 'The sacrifices of God are a broken spirit; a broken and a contrite heart, O God, you will not despise.'

God doesn't like a proud heart. Perhaps when things were better for you, you were arrogant, you were not approachable, you were not teachable. People had to tiptoe around you. God looked down from heaven and said of you, 'I love him. I've got great plans for him, but I can't use him right now. In order to bring him to where I want him to be, I am going to have to deal with him.'

In the case of Job, we are told at the beginning of the book that he was 'blameless and upright. He feared God and shunned evil.' Maybe that isn't the case with you; you are far from blameless, far from upright. But God still loves you. Sometimes God will take a person, who may seem blameless, but God knows what is in his or her heart. God also knows what is in your heart. Whether you are a decent person like Job, or you have reached the bottom (because of your lack of morals or the way you have abused your body or the lies you have told about people or your corrupt financial dealings), God loves you.

Then you begin to think, 'Why would God love me?' I don't know, but he does. But has he got your attention? Have you begun to pray with tears?

The third way we know that God is on our case is when we *cry for mercy* (verse 2).

Has your attitude towards God been one of thinking that because you gave up this and did that, God has to bless you? When you come to understand the God of the Bible, you will realize he is sovereign. He may give you mercy or he may not.

When you ask for mercy, it is because you are at the bottom. You have reached such a low plain, it is all you can do. When God is on your case you come to realize that you have no bargaining power, and you begin to ask for mercy.

Fourthly we know God is on our case when we *see our sin*: 'If you, O LORD, kept a record of sins, O Lord, who could stand?' (verse 3). Until we are in this position, we have had no conviction of sin at all.

This is what happens to the backslider. The backslider begins to do things that he was saved from, falling back into old habits, and losing his sense of sin. Spiritual blindness comes over him, and he becomes unteachable and unreachable. In order to get his attention, God has to bring him right down.

When God is on your case, he begins to deal with you. You may appear to be upright and blameless like Job, but if God wanted to show you what you really are like, he could find something in you very quickly. You can wear a mask and convince everybody around you that you are like Job, but God knows what you really are like. When he puts his magnifying glass on your heart, you understand why the psalmist said, 'Lord, if you kept a record of sins, who could stand?'

Do you think you are an exception to this? Do you think you are different, that you could stand before God without blushing? Let me ask you, if God were to flash all your thoughts on a giant screen for all who know you to see, would you get a little nervous? Would you like all you have ever said or thought about others to be unveiled? The truth is, God has kept a record; it will be unveiled one day – unless you have found his forgiveness in advance of that Day.

You know God is on your case when you find you are struggling to come to terms with the fact that inside of you is a little Adolf Hitler!

Fifthly, we know that God is on our case when we confess to him what is revealed to us. One of the greatest verses in the Bible is 1 John 1:9: 'If we confess our sins, he is faithful and just and will forgive us our sins and purify us from all unrighteousness.' Something happened to the psalmist between verses 3 and 4, because having just said, 'If you kept a record of sin, who could stand?' he then continues, 'But with you there is forgiveness.'

There is nothing greater than having God forgive you. At the end of the day all that matters is to know that he forgives us. When God is on our case, we begin to see how vile we have been. We think, 'Why is he showing me my sin like this?' God doesn't bring us face to face with our sin only to make us feel awful. No, the Holy Spirit convicts not only of sin, but also of righteousness. This means that the Holy Spirit shows us what Jesus did for us, that all of our sins have been paid for by the blood that Jesus shed on the cross of Calvary.

So we confess what God has shown to us. The result is that we fear God. The reason why we sin as we do is because there is no sense of the fear of God. It doesn't bother us, but when God is on our case, suddenly we are scared to sin. Today, there is a such a flippant attitude towards God. But the God of the Bible hates sin.

Sixthly, we know that God is on our case when we get an appreciation for his Word: 'I wait for the LORD, my soul waits, and in his word I put my hope' (verse 5). The Bible is God's Word and it is the truth. When God is on our case we begin to appreciate this. God has magnified his Word above his name (Psalm 138:2). God will honour you to the degree you honour his Word: 'Them that honour me, I will honour' (1 Samuel 2:30).

The seventh way we know that God is on our case is described in verse 6: 'My soul waits for the Lord more than watchmen wait for the morning.' *God brings us* to a new level of expectancy. Look at what the psalmist says: 'My soul waits for the Lord,' *just* for the Lord.

When God is on our case he wants to bring us to the place where he matters more than anything in the world; he wants each of us all to himself.

Years ago, Louise and I were given tickets to sit in a box in the Royal Albert Hall. My first reaction was, 'Honey, who shall we invite to go with us?' Louise replied, 'You want to invite somebody; I thought just you and I would go. I thought that maybe you would like just to be with me!' I knew what she meant. And God's like that. When he is on your case he brings you to a new level of expectancy. That expectancy is the joy of his presence alone. Just him. Alone. How much? 'More than watchmen wait for the morning.'

We have been looking at seven ways that we can know if God is on our case. What is behind all this? It is that God wants to take us over completely: 'O Israel, put your hope in the LORD, for with the LORD is unfailing love and with him is full redemption. He himself will redeem Israel from all their sins.' The word *redeem* means 'to buy back'. God is our Creator, but the human race fell when Adam sinned in the Garden of Eden. We ran from God, but he wanted us so much he bought us back, bought us with the price of the blood of his Son.

A number of years ago, I knew of a little boy who was given a block of balsa wood out of which he made a boat. It had taken him weeks, but it was the envy of many people who saw it. He noticed one day it was missing. And it broke his heart, for he loved that boat.

A few weeks later he was walking down the street and he looked in the window of a second-hand shop. There was his boat for sale. He went in and said to the owner, 'That's my boat in the window!' The man said, 'It's not your boat! It's my boat. Someone brought it in and I bought it. Do you want to buy it? That's the only way you are going to get it.'

The boy went home, scraped up every penny he had and went back to the shop and bought his boat. As he took his boat home he talked to it. He said, 'Once I owned you because I made you. Now I own you because I bought you.' And that is what God is saying to us, 'Once I owned you because I made you. But now I own you because I have bought you.'

God is on your case. He wants to take you over because you are his.

12

Psalm 131

The mother of all battles

My heart is not proud, O LORD,
    my eyes are not haughty;
I do not concern myself with great matters
    or things too wonderful for me.

But I have stilled and quietened my soul;
    like a weaned child with its mother,
    like a weaned child is my soul within me.

O Israel, put your hope in the LORD
    both now and for evermore.

Psalm 131 is an extraordinary Psalm of David. When we read the opening words, 'My heart is not proud, O LORD, my eyes are not haughty', we want to ask, 'Whoever could make a statement like that!'

Remember the Bible says that 'the heart is deceitful above all things and desperately wicked; who can know it?' (Jeremiah 17:9, *AV*). 'My eyes are not haughty' – surely it is a proud person who would talk like this. At first glance this is what I thought.

What did David mean? If he is telling the truth, we are seeing a quality of humility that is very rare. What a contrast to the spirit of today! We are living in an age in which we must catch the eye of other people. The key to success today has mainly to do with pride and self-esteem.

But the key to success in the world is the way of disaster in the things of the Spirit. There are many Christians today whose real problem is their pride. They want to be greater than others. This is in contrast to what Jesus said to his disciples: 'The greatest among you will be your servant. For whoever exalts himself will be humbled, and whoever humbles himself will be exalted' (Matthew 23:11-12).

Some people have motivation but they don't have ability; others have a lot of ability but they don't have motivation. David had both. He was a highly motivated man, with outstanding ability. He was a military genius, defeating his country's enemies and capturing Jerusalem. He lived each day in high gear, from the moment he woke up until he went to sleep at night.

But when David wanted to build a temple for his God, God would not let him because he was a warrior and had shed blood (1 Chronicles 28:3). David must have felt a little hurt.

I suspect that he may have been similarly hurt when Samuel came to the house of David's father Jesse to anoint the one who was to follow Saul as king. Samuel saw six sons, but did not see the one whom God had chosen. Only when David, the youngest son, who had been looking after the sheep, was brought in did Samuel realize that David was God's choice. David must have felt hurt that his own father didn't see much in him.

In addition, we know from a previous incident recorded in 1 Samuel 17 that there was sibling rivalry in his family. When Israel was fighting the Philistines, David went to see how his brothers were doing on the battlefield. He discovered that the Israelites were frightened of a giant called Goliath. David did not think the giant should be a problem to God's people, but David's brothers thought he was conceited. So, on the one hand, his father did not appreciate him; and on the other, his brothers made fun of him. When a person grows up in that kind of atmosphere, it can either be the death of him or the making of him. In David's case it made him want to amount to something.

Maybe you have been stepped on or walked over and for a time felt very sorry for yourself. But you were determined that it would not destroy you. So you thought, 'I'm going to show them what I can do.' David was that way. I think that is partly why he was so motivated.

Christians can be motivated for wrong reasons. A businessman can sit through the whole of a church service with his mind on a deal that he is about to make. An insurance salesman can look over the congregation to see if there is anyone present who would be likely to want a policy. But motivation is not limited to secular callings. It is possible to be in the ministry and call it work for God, when in fact the motivation is personal pride.

However, something happened to David, for he could say,

'My heart is not proud, O LORD,
    my eyes are not haughty;
I do not concern myself with great matters,
    or things too wonderful for me.
But I have stilled and quieted my soul;
    like a weaned child with its mother.
    Like a weaned child is my soul within me.'

When did David write these words?

Some say it was in old age that he mellowed. I hope not. Are we to believe that the only thing that mellows a person is old age? I don't think so. Something spiritual happened to David.

Perhaps it happened when he came to terms with Nathan's word informing him that he could not build the temple. The Chronicler records how David came to terms with this restriction:

> Then King David went in and sat before the LORD, and he said: 'Who am I, O LORD God, and what is my family, that you have brought me this far? And as if this were not enough in your sight, O God, you have spoken about the future of the house of your servant. You have looked on me as though I were the most exalted of men, O LORD God. What more can David say to you for honouring your servant? For you know your servant' (1 Chronicles 17:16-18).

John Newton wrote a hymn every week, and he would base the hymn on the verse from which he was going to preach. One week he was due to preach on these words, 'Who am I, O LORD God, and what is my family that you have brought me thus far?', and it was then that he wrote the hymn 'Amazing Grace'. John Newton realized what God had done for him.

And David realized what God had done for him. It may have been at the very moment of refusal by God that David came to terms with the fact that, although God had been so good to him, there were some things he was not to do.

This is a problem many people face; they can never have enough. I have never understood why a millionaire wants his second million. No matter how successful some people are, they always think a little bit more will finally make them happy.

Another possible event that caused David to become in his own words 'as a weaned child' could be his sin with Bathsheba. I would lean towards this event. David committed adultery, then he tried to cover it up with murder. David was forgiven but he would reap the consequence of his sin: the sword would not leave his house.

When I preached through the life of David, I did not want to continue after his fall because of the judgment that came to his family. I lacked the motivation to go on preaching on his life.

It so happened that this coincided with my church's first day of prayer and fasting. I never will forget it. It was one of those rare moments when the Lord spoke so clearly to me.

He said, 'Don't you know that that's where most of your people are? Most of your people have some sin, some disgrace, some skeleton in the cupboard, and the outlook is bleak for them. Are you to say

that the only kind of preaching you should do is
when somebody is on top?'

I felt really smitten and convicted. I continued
with the life of David. I don't know if the church
would agree with me, but I thought the best preaching on the life of David occurred after that. I began to see something of the man. He was so humbled.

Therefore I think it was his fall and restoration
that led David to write this psalm. He had come to
terms with what really mattered, had come to terms
with himself and with his God. He proclaimed, as
someone once put it, an armistice in the civil war
of his emotions. It was a kind of spiritual rebirth.
What a pity it took what he went through to bring
him to that!

Dr Carl F. H. Henry is a great man of God, as
well as one of the most scholarly men of our century. He has written dozens of books, and was a
co-founder of *Christianity Today* with Billy Graham. I can remember being with him near Buckingham Palace, heading towards Westminster
Chapel. I asked him, 'Carl, if you had your life to
live over, what would you do differently?' He
thought, and then said, 'I would remember that only
God can turn the water into wine.'

I knew exactly what he meant.

We can say that in our heads, but it is more
difficult to live with it in our hearts. Psalm 131

shows a man who is starting out all over again.

There are similarities with David's words in Psalm 51, after Nathan the prophet had convicted him of his adultery.

> Create in me a pure heart, O God,
>   and renew a steadfast spirit within me.
> Do not cast me from your presence
>   or take your Holy Spirit from me.
> Restore to me the joy of your salvation
>   and grant me a willing spirit, to sustain me.

Then he goes on to say,

> The sacrifices of God are a broken spirit;
>   a broken and contrite heart,
>   O God, you will not despise.
>   (Psalm 51:10-12,17)

Something happened to David. It was a spiritual rebirth. God calmed his soul. He found that peace of mind is more desirable than worldly success. He was as happy as a little baby, weaned but still leaning against his mother's breast.

The most perfect contentment in all the human race is the weaned baby on his mother's breast. At the start of the weaning process the baby feels a sense of rejection, but after it is weaned it is able to lay its head on its mother's breast, knowing that it is accepted and feeling peace and joy.

David may have felt a rejection from God, for he was chastened for his sin. But God loved him. In the latter part of David's life, success was sometimes out of the question; but he began to know God intimately, and that's when many of the Psalms were written.

You too can know God intimately. Whatever failure you have experienced or whatever guilt you carry, it is not too late for you. Now is the time to begin to live.

The greatest battle we face is not what happened in the Gulf or in the Falklands or in Korea. The greatest battle is described in Galatians 5:17: 'For the sinful nature desires what is contrary to the Spirit, and the Spirit what is contrary to the sinful nature. They are in conflict with each other.'

What is the mother of battles? Pride. There is the pride of ambition, the need to be seen with the right people. Do you know what causes sexual lust? It is pride; the need to be accepted by the opposite sex. It is pride that leads to adultery and sexual immorality. Why do we experience jealousy? It is pride. Why do we want more and more? It is pride. Why is it we cannot forgive a person? It is pride. What makes us point the finger? It is pride.

Our pride will cause us to do stupid things. It will delay us coming to terms with the most important thing in the world; our relationship with

God himself. Pride keeps a person from confessing Christ openly, from going out on the streets to witness.

Jesus bore the sin of our pride at Calvary. He knew humiliation. He was naked on the cross. When we see all that the Son of God went through, we must know that there was no other way whereby we could be saved. It is not by our good works. It is not by our joining a church. It is not by our stopping this or that habit, however bad it is.

Something will happen to us when we resign from the rat-race and realize that the only thing that matters is for God to have us all to himself. We will get to know him and we will be amazed.

Remember, the key to success in the world is the way of disaster in the things of the Spirit.

13

Psalm 132

How to cope with hardships

O LORD, remember David
　　and all the hardships he endured.

He swore an oath to the LORD
　　and made a vow to the Mighty One of Jacob:
'I will not enter my house
　　or go to my bed –
I will allow no sleep to my eyes,
　　no slumber to my eyelids,
till I find a place for the LORD,
　　a dwelling for the Mighty One of Jacob.'

We heard it in Ephrathah,
　　we came upon it in the fields of Jaar:
'Let us go to his dwelling place;
　　let us worship at his footstool –
arise, O LORD, and come to your resting place,
　　you and the ark of your might.
May your priests be clothed with righteousness;
　　may your saints sing for joy.'

For the sake of David your servant.
　　do not reject your anointed one.

The LORD swore an oath to David,
    a sure oath that he will not revoke:
'One of your own descendants
    I will place on your throne –
if your sons keep my covenant
    and the statutes I teach them,
then their sons will sit
    on your throne for ever and ever.'

For the LORD has chosen Zion,
    he has desired it for his dwelling:
'This is my resting place for ever and ever;
    here I will sit enthroned, for I have desired it –
I will bless her with abundant provisions;
    her poor will I satisfy with food.
I will clothe her priests with salvation,
    and her saints will ever sing for joy.

'Here I will make a horn grow for David
    and set up a lamp for my anointed one.
I will clothe his enemies with shame,
    but the crown on his head will be resplendent.'

Psalm 132 shows how to cope with hardships: 'O LORD, remember David and all the hardships he endured.' When people think of King David, they normally recall his conquering Jerusalem, uniting the kingdom and bringing the Ark to Jerusalem. David was Israel's greatest king.

But this psalm refers to something not often thought about: the hardships he endured. It is also a psalm that refers to swearing an oath. Do you know what an oath is? It is a promise with a guarantee that it will take place.

There are two references to oaths in this psalm. The first is what David swore to the Lord (verse 2); the second is what the Lord swore to David (verse 11).

The Old Testament used 'oath' interchangeably with 'vow'. What is the difference between a promise and a vow or oath? The latter are stronger. There are warnings in the Old Testament about breaking a vow: 'When you make a vow to God, do not delay in fulfilling it. He has no pleasure in fools; fulfil your vow. It is better not to vow than to make a vow and not fulfil it' (Ecclesiastes 5:4-5).

Psalm 132 describes an occasion when David swore an oath to the Lord. He said, 'I will not enter my house or go to my bed. I will allow no sleep to my eyes, no slumber to my eyelids, till I find a place for the LORD, a dwelling for the mighty one of Jacob.'

His oath could refer to the temple that David wanted to build, a vow that he was not able to keep. This may have been partly what was meant by the hardships of David.

Let us go on to look at some of the other hardships he endured.

David was not appreciated at home
We touched on this first hardship in the previous chapter; his father overlooked him and his brothers mocked him. Perhaps your problem is that due to a faulty relationship with your family, there is a bruise upon your soul, a hurt in your emotions. You have never recovered from the hardship brought on you by those that should have been closest to you.

It is interesting that David was a failure as a father, and experienced much heartache over his own family. It may be that you are feeling this kind of deep hurt because you know you are not the kind of parent or brother or sister you should be. David, though he was Israel's greatest king, privately knew a depth of sorrow that people do not often think about.

David wasn't appreciated by his king
This second hardship made life very difficult. Saul, David's king, was subject to periods of demonic influence. Whenever an evil spirit came upon Saul,

David, a gifted musician, would play his harp and relief would come to Saul (1 Samuel 16:14-23).

But, David became a popular general because of his victories over the Philistines. The people danced and sang, 'Saul has slain his thousands, David his tens of thousands.' Saul was very angry at this refrain and kept a jealous eye on David (1 Samuel 18:1-9). Here was David's new employer watching him. David was not only unappreciated, he was feared.

Is there a sense in which this could relate to you? Maybe you are not appreciated at work, the conditions in the office are so oppressive and so difficult that it is all you can think about. You can let your situation throw you and become your downfall, or you can accept it as being part of God's preparation for you and allow it to turn you into one of the strongest human beings that ever lived. That's what happened to David.

David had to wait for God
This third hardship must really have tested David's faith: he had to wait for years before what was promised to him was fulfilled. After being anointed as king, he wasn't immediately made king; it was only a word from God. David was still subject to Saul and had to flee from him. His anointing seemed to bring nothing but trouble.

It may be that God gave you hope at some time

in the past, but now you are perplexed. Perhaps someone that you trusted gave you a word to encourage you. Perhaps at some stage in your life God himself manifested his power and you knew you had a sure word from him. There is not a single Christian who, at one time or another, doesn't know the feeling of God speaking to him or her. Then a year goes by, and you begin to think, 'Lord, did you really speak to me?' David had to wait for years before what was promised to him was fulfilled.

One thing you can do while you are waiting, is to submit to everything God allows to happen. All of these hardships David endured were part of his preparation.

You may think you are beyond that stage of being prepared because of your age! C. H. Spurgeon, the great preacher of the nineteenth century, late in life said: 'If I knew I had twenty-five years left, I would spent twenty of it in preparation.'

Many people today, especially young people, want everything right now. They don't want to be prepared.

I went through this years ago myself. I thought, 'Why do I need to go back to seminary and university?' Louise and I had been married for twelve years when I felt I had to go back and get more education. And I thought, 'Why should I do anything like this?'

But we came to England and I spent three years studying at Oxford, before I was called to Westminster Chapel at the age of forty-one. At the time I thought, 'I have a university research degree behind me. Now I am prepared, now I am ready!' But do you know, I would say that 95% of my ministry in the Chapel has been God preparing me for something.

Preparation is not always pleasant. God will put you through delayed vindication and unanswered prayer; it is not easy.

David fell into great sin

Nothing is so surprising as the experience of this man who ascended to such heights, but who let sexual sin bring him right down (2 Samuel 11-12). But God is no respecter of persons. He will not bend the rules because of who you are. David was a man after God's own heart, but God wouldn't bend the rules for him. This fourth hardship was his own fault.

Making a vow that you cannot keep

David swore an oath to the Lord, and it turned out that he was not able to keep it. In all probability it refers to his desire to build a temple for the Lord.

We can make a vow that is not precipitated by the Holy Spirit, a vow that God is not in.

One of the saddest stories in the Bible is that of

Jephthah in Judges 11. Jephthah made a vow to the Lord that if God give him victory over the Ammonites, he would sacrifice as a burnt offering whatever came out of the door of his house to meet him when he returned in triumph. When Jephthah returned to his home, who should come out to meet him but his daughter, dancing to the sound of tambourines.

What are we to say about Jephthah's vow? Basically he should never have made it. A vow that is not under the leadership of the Holy Spirit can result only in a feeling of guilt and regret.

Many people, when in a religious mood, will make a vow to God. There is a place in California where returning missionaries come for rest. Sometimes they need counselling for depression. In many cases, they went to the mission field because of a vow made when they were children which they felt they had to keep. Years later they realized God had not called them. The reason for their difficulty was a vow.

Perhaps you are in a similar situation, overcome with guilt because of something you vowed to do. It could be that which is bringing you great hardship.

The Lord's vow to David
There is nothing more wonderful than the knowledge that comes when the Lord swears an oath to

you. He does it in such a way that you never doubt
he is going to keep his word.

Whereas a promise in almost every case is based
upon a condition, an oath is not. God didn't just
promise to David, he swore an oath to him that
from the fruit of his loins would come the Lord
Jesus Christ.

David was not worthy for God to use him because of his sins of adultery and murder. But he
married Bathsheba and they had a son Solomon.
Although God had many options from the fruit of
David's loins from which to choose the line of the
promised Messiah, God worked through Solomon,
the son of the woman with whom David committed adultery. If we were planning this, we would
have said, 'The blood line of the Messiah cannot
go through Solomon.'

We should be encouraged to know that whatever hardship we have gone through, even if the
hardship was our own fault, God can take our life
and work all over again and, at the end of the day,
make everything look as though it is the way it
was supposed to be.

How do we cope with hardships? We have two
choices: either we trust our vow to God, which in
the end will give us more bondage and more guilt
when we inevitably let God down, or we can trust
God's vow to us. We should trust his word.

God's commitment to the blood of Jesus

Psalm 132 says that the Lord has chosen Zion and has desired it for his dwelling place. This is a reference to the Ark of the Covenant. It was just a little chest with a gold lid, and on that gold lid the High Priest sprinkled blood from an animal to atone for sin. God committed himself to that blood. Every person who gives up hope of being saved by their personal works or by keeping their vows discovers that rest and joy come to those who trust God's vow to them.

God has committed himself irrevocably to the blood Jesus shed on the cross of Calvary. There is an old spiritual: 'Were you there when they crucified my Lord? Were you there?' I can tell you, had you been there you would not have seen a thing – only a ghastly crucifixion. There was no hint that the blood dripping from Jesus' head, hands and feet was the most precious commodity in the history of the world. More precious than the gold and diamonds of South Africa, more precious than the Queen's jewels – is the very blood that was spilt on Good Friday. Why? That blood *satisfied* the justice of God. 'When I see the blood, I will pass over you', God continues to say when people transfer the hope they had in their own efforts to what Jesus did for them on the cross.

If you are the greatest of sinners, whatever your sin may be, God has so committed himself to the blood of Jesus Christ that if you repent, you will receive a pardon that is categorical and total and complete, as though you had never sinned. This is the scandal of the Christian faith.

God will take your past, whatever the hardships, and work it for good.

14

Psalm 133

The unity of the Spirit

How good and pleasant it is
　　when brothers live together in unity!
It is like precious oil poured on the head,
　　running down on the beard,
running down on Aaron's beard,
　　down upon the collar of his robes.
It is as if the dew of Hermon
　　were falling on Mount Zion.
For there the LORD bestows his blessing,
　　even life for evermore.

This particular Psalm of Ascent was written by David who, better than most, knew what it was like to have a rival spirit in Israel.

In Ephesians 4:2-3, which is a parallel passage, Paul the apostle puts it like this: 'Be completely humble and gentle; be patient, bearing with one another in love. Make every effort to keep the unity of the Spirit through the bond of peace.' Why would Paul even need to talk about the unity of the Spirit?

Is the Holy Spirit divided within himself? The Holy Spirit lives in believers. If Christians are not speaking, then the Spirit is divided. And that's the point. The Holy Spirit himself is torn between his people if believers are divided.

It is interesting that Ephesians 4, which is an unusual chapter, begins and ends with references to the Holy Spirit. It begins by referring to the unity of the Spirit; it ends with the reference to grieving the Spirit. It is so easy for the Holy Spirit to be grieved. And so Paul says, 'And do not grieve the Holy Spirit of God, with whom you were sealed for the day of redemption' (Ephesians 4:30).

If we come together and the Holy Spirit is grieved, then it should not surprise us if he does not work in a powerful manner. Unity of the Spirit is found when he is in each of us, ungrieved.

They say in the hills of Kentucky, 'The God that's in me won't fight the God that's in you.' The ungrieved Spirit in me will recognize the ungrieved

Spirit in you. The Holy Spirit recognizes himself.

It is a wonderful fellowship when each believer knows the ungrieved Spirit at work. When we are together the unity compounds and the fellowship is incredible. That's the way it was in the early church. They were together of one accord at Pentecost. Sometime later, in Acts 4, the Spirit came down and they were all of one heart and one soul. It is wonderful when it is like that.

The unity of the Spirit is a remarkable achievement. Why? Because it goes right against human nature. Everyone in the body of Christ on earth is a sinner.

We all have our opinions, and we are sure that we are right. And right beside our opinion is our pride. If I hold to a particular point of view then my pride is at stake if you don't go along with me. It is natural for me to want to be proved right, to have my opinion validated. So I want you to agree with me. If you do agree with me, I like it. But the fact that I want it doesn't mean that it's right.

Because we are all sinners, it is not surprising when there is tension. It is not surprising when a church is divided with rivalry.

The unity of the Spirit is not natural, but it is supernatural, therefore it cannot be explained naturally. What do I mean by that?

When a boy and a girl fall in love – that's natural; we can understand because it has a natural explanation. When we come across a person who is ambitious to achieve, we can understand this too, because this also is natural. It is natural for a person born and bred in Britain to speak with a British accent. It is natural for people to recover from illness; medical people tell me that 85 per cent of all sicknesses would get better anyway, without medicine.

But unity of the Spirit is supernatural. It means that our natural ways, where we want to be heard and make our opinion felt, are not important, and we are willing to climb down.

Before I came to Westminster Chapel, I was pastor of a little American church, near the Upper Heyford airforce base. On one occasion I had as a guest preacher a man by the name of Clive Francisco. He was Old Testament Professor at my seminary in Louisville, and he preached for me for a week.

During that week, one of the members of the church, an army master-sergeant who always had his way, had his feelings hurt. I told Dr Francisco about it and we went to the man's house. The man was full of himself because he had probably been mistreated, and what he wanted he didn't get.

Dr Francisco had such wisdom and gentleness that the army sergeant broke down and wept; his shoulders shook and he said, 'I'm sorry!' Dr Francisco said to me later, 'That's one of the greatest miracles of the Spirit that I've seen in years, for a person to admit that his attitude was wrong.'

What Dr Francisco did was to come alongside this man in the spirit of Galatians 6:1, 'Brothers, if someone is caught in a sin, you who are spiritual should restore him gently. But watch yourself, or you also may be tempted.'

How good and pleasant it is

What does it take for brothers to dwell together in unity?

Firstly, there must be the willingness to lose face. This means doing without being openly seen to have been right, and getting our own way. This is why unity of the Spirit is a remarkable achievement – in order for it to happen, somebody has to be willing to lose face.

Unity almost always means compromise. There are those who say, 'I will not compromise, I am standing for our precious truth.' I suspect that when we get to heaven we will discover that 98 per cent of the theological controversies in the history of the Christian church had nothing to do with theology at all. When people speak of holding to principles, often it is personal. It is so easy to take that line. But compromise is not a bad word; it means a climbdown. It means saying either, 'I was wrong', or, 'Your way, I believe, is better.' We realize that what we thought was important is not as important as having peace.

Secondly, to achieve unity there must be the will to forgive and forget. I can choose to forgive or I can choose to hold a grudge. By nature, I want to hold a grudge. I want to have scope to be able to point the finger, but if I forgive you, I can no longer point the finger. This is why unity doesn't take place. Somebody won't forgive and forget.

But forgiving and forgetting is not something we do only once, it is something we are to keep on doing. There are five principles of total forgiveness, based on Genesis 45:1-15:

1: You will not let anybody know what they did to you. Joseph put all but his brothers out of the room so that nobody in Egypt would know what they did to him. Joseph hid their sin from the people, just like God hides our sin.

2: You will not punish through fear, or let anybody be intimidated or scared to death. Joseph didn't want his brothers to be afraid of him. When we want another to feel intimidated it is because we haven't totally forgiven him or her.

3: You will not let that person be angry with himself for what he has done. You want him to forgive himself.

4: You want that person to save face. Joseph

ensured this by showing God's sovereign purpose; God was behind all that happened, so
don't feel guilty!

5: You refuse to blackmail that person by threat-
ening to tell what you know to another person
who is a key figure.

We should be like Joseph when he forgave his
brothers. He didn't want anybody to know what
his brothers had done to him; he didn't want his
brothers to be afraid of him; he didn't want his
brothers to be angry with themselves for what they
had done; he wanted them to save face, so he said
it wasn't them who sent him to Egypt, it was God;
he wouldn't let them tell their father, Jacob, what
they had done.

Total forgiveness is when you protect the other
person.

But there is a sixth principle: forgiving and forgetting is something we keep on doing. In the case
of Joseph and his brothers, seventeen years later,
after Jacob's death, the brothers thought that Joseph
would punish them. But they found out that seventeen years on he still forgave them (Genesis
50:15-21).

We are to keep it up; to forgive and to forget.
God does that, and we are to forgive one another
as God has forgiven us.

Unity is remarkable, thirdly, because in honour believers really do prefer one another. They have the will not to take the credit. There is a reason for Billy Graham's success in Britain that very few know about. It has almost entirely to do with an evangelist, now in Heaven, by the name of Tom Rees. Until Billy's arrival in 1954 the best known evangelist in Britain was Tom Rees, who regularly filled the Royal Albert Hall with his meetings. But he abandoned these in order to push Billy. He used his influence and friends to make the way for Billy, not unlike John the Baptist pointing people to Christ. Tom Rees literally did that regarding Billy Graham. Billy would not have been so successful had not Tom Rees stepped to one side.

Like precious oil poured on the head

Unity is a remarkable achievement and comes as a result of the awareness that the anointing is primary. This is the thrust of Psalm 133. David said that unity is like precious oil, poured out on the head. The word 'oil' implies anointing. It is the Holy Spirit that is symbolized by the oil.

Aaron's robe was ornate: 'Make the ephod of gold, and of blue, purple and scarlet yarn, and of finely twisted linen – the work of a skilled craftsman' (Exodus 28:6). Can you imagine how the person who was chosen to make that robe, felt when he saw oil being poured on it? But, according to David, more beautiful than the robe or the beard was the oil.

This beauty was not just because the oil had a pleasant scent. Comprised of myrrh, cinnamon, and other spices it would have had a very lovely smell. But what mattered was the anointing.

I have had to come to this in my preaching. There are times in my preparation when I think, 'How will this sound?' But then I think, 'Is that following the Spirit?' The point is, is the preacher willing, after he has prepared his sermon, to go to the pulpit and forget its effects, in order for the anointing to flow?

Many in the ministry work hard on their sermons, selecting what points to stress and how to say them. Then during the sermon they think, 'I've got a feeling I ought to say this.' But then they think, 'No, I'm not going to say this because I'm not going to be able to make this point I have studied all week.'

With regard to unity, are we willing for the messiness of our appearance to come through? Or must we look good? Must we save face? But David said, 'Beautiful though Aaron's robe is, there is something lovelier than it, and it is the oil that is running down to his collar.'

What Psalm 133 is stressing is the priority of the anointing. This remarkable achievement, called the unity of the Spirit, comes as a result of seeing the anointing as primary. David had come to the place where he saw that it is not the beauty of the beard, it is not the beauty of the robe, it is the oil! The unity of the brothers is better than all that seems so beautiful.

We should be willing to stand back and allow the Spirit to flow. A person causes disunity when he or she says, 'You're not taking notice of the point I'm wanting to make and my view hasn't really been aired.' But there is something more beautiful than my opinion or my sermon or my point of view, and that is for the Spirit to flow.

The presence of the Holy Spirit has a wonderful effect. When the Spirit is grieved, feelings are so acute and our opinions matter so much, that we are at one another's throats, pointing the finger and wanting our way.

During the Cane Ridge Revival in 1800 in Kentucky, the Baptists, the Methodists, the Presbyterians and the Episcopalians were at each other's throats. The Baptists insisted on eternal security; the Methodists stated it was possible to lose one's salvation; the Episcopalians were concerned with the primacy of the episcopacy and their ecclesiology; the Presbyterians wanted to uphold their form of government. There was denominational rivalry.

At the height of the Cane Ridge Revival, when the Spirit was powerful, the sound of people praising God and praying to him was as loud as Niagara. The sound could be heard a mile away. And those denominational differences dissolved, and were replaced by a love for one another. People were converted. Strong men would come to the area hoping to ruin the revival, but the power was so great they found themselves on their knees, and were converted. The momentum lasted for quite a while. But at the height, all those differences just meant nothing.

When the Spirit is absent, our opinions mean so much to us. But when there is power, people will honour Jesus.

On one occasion when Evangelist Glen Griffith held a series of evangelistic meetings in Ashland, Kentucky, he preached for two weeks. His preaching was wonderful, and every sermon was better than the previous one. Just like a builder laying bricks, he went higher and higher.

Then came the last night. The place was packed, but Glen Griffith just stood there. Tears started to roll down his cheeks and he began to sing a chorus: 'Wonderful! Wonderful! Jesus is to me. Counsellor, Prince of peace, mighty God is he.' I wanted him to stop singing and get on with his sermon. But he sang it again and then he sang it a third time.

People rose out of their seats and within five minutes forty people were down at the front on their knees. He never preached that evening.

He had prepared a sermon, but he realized the priority of the anointing. He gave in to it rather than preach his sermon. This is what is meant by 'honour the blood and honour the Holy Ghost', as R.T. Williams used to say.

There are three observations that I suggest are important.

Firstly, *blessing is given where there is unity*: 'For there the LORD bestows his blessing.'

Secondly, *unity is what Satan fears most*. Along the way he will put ideas in your mind, he will come alongside like an angel of light to make you think something is of the Lord when it is not. The devil will remind you of every wrong in other people.

Thirdly, *unity of the Spirit is not an optional matter*. We have to have it in order to survive. Some of us have lost credibility where we live because we have to have our way all the time, and people feel they are walking on eggshells because we are so difficult and so abrasive. What we need to do is to come to the place where the Holy Spirit is un-grieved, and we are willing to feel messy and not look so good; then the anointing will flow.

15

Psalm 134

The minister and the ministry

Praise the LORD, all you servants of the LORD
  who minister by night in the house of the LORD,
Lift up your hands in the sanctuary
  and praise the LORD.

May the LORD, the Maker of heaven and earth,
  bless you from Zion.

This psalm is about those called to minister: 'Praise the LORD, all you servants of the LORD who minister by night in the house of the LORD', and my subject is *the minister and the ministry*.

The 'house of the Lord' in verse 1 probably refers to the temple and the servants would be the priests and Levites. Those who were born in the tribe of Levi were from birth set apart for ministry in the house of the Lord. The Book of Leviticus gives details of the ceremonial law and the way the worship of God was carried out in Israel. It was the task of the priests and Levites to carry out the worship of God. They were doing what they were called to do. That is my first reason for dealing with this subject.

But another reason is that it is a subject which needs examining from time to time. All Christians need to be reminded periodically of the elementary principles concerning the minister and the ministry. Then they will understand what is meant by the ministry, and will have an appreciation of it.

I think there are two tragedies in our generation. One is that there are many in the ministry who have not been called of God, and the other is that there are many out of the ministry who have spurned the call of God. It may be that what I write will cause somebody with whom the Lord has been dealing to think very carefully about this matter. It is a great honour whenever I discover someone who is called to the ministry under my own ministry.

This psalm, therefore, doesn't refer to all believers. I had thought that it could, but to be fair, I doubt it because, even though all Christians are servants of the Lord in a sense, the psalm refers to those who are set apart in a special manner.

There are three things from this psalm which I want to look at in the course of this final chapter: the man who is called to the ministry; the ministry and the mandate given to it; the ministry and the mystery.

The man who is called to the ministry

There are certain assumptions regarding such men in Psalm 134.

I have already mentioned one; he would be a Levite. Only those descended from Levi could work in the temple. They had no material inheritance, for we read in Deuteronomy 10:9: 'That is why the Levites have no share or inheritance among their brothers; the LORD is their inheritance, as the LORD your God told them'; and in Numbers 26:62: 'All the male Levites a month old or more, numbered 23,000. They were not counted along with the other Israelites because they received no inheritance among them.'

The application for today is that believers are *not to enter the ministry for material benefit*. I have never understood why it is that some manage to do so and get away with it. This applies especially to those who preach the Health and Wealth gospel. I know of one such minister in Florida who, when he felt convicted about owning a Rolls Royce, sold it and bought a Mercedes instead! I know another famous likeable minister who became a millionaire as a result of being in a certain church in America where well-heeled deacons advised him where to invest money. But if *you* are thinking about going into the ministry, don't plan to be a millionaire or drive a Mercedes.

Another assumption in this psalm is that those serving in the temple *were men and not women*. The New Testament continues the Old Testament assumption that 'called' men are in charge of the things of God.

I have just mentioned a third assumption; the Levites *were called by God*. They didn't ask to be Levites. Today, when a person is called by God, he can argue with the Lord, but the Levites could not. The psalm shows that a person was there not of his own choosing. The ministry only includes those who are called.

It is not wrong to want to go into the ministry, because that could be God's way of calling you. I had that problem myself. I wanted to be a preacher when I was a child, but I would hear different ministers warn young men, 'Don't you dare go into the ministry unless you are called!' And I thought,

'I'm still waiting for that calling.'

One of my best friends said that the Lord spoke to him with an audible voice and called him by name and said, 'Go, preach!' And he just said, 'Yes, Lord, I will!' I found out later he was standing right next to me when it occurred. And I wanted something similar to happen to me.

I heard of another person who, when he was ploughing corn in his field, saw clouds in the formation 'GP', which he believed was the Lord saying, 'Go, Preach!' Those who heard him decided that what it was saying was, 'Go, Plough!' But I never had anything like that happen to me. And I was just waiting for the call.

I went away to Treveca, planning to be a lawyer. Then God sent a Scotsman, John Sutherland Logan, across the Atlantic. When I heard him preach I knew it was the greatest sermon I had ever heard. I heard him a second time and it was better. I got to know him a bit, and I asked, 'How will I know if I am ever called?' He looked at me and said, 'You are!' I said, 'How do I know?' He spent time with me and convinced me that I was, and I felt that he was telling me the truth.

What disappointed me was that it was so unsensational; there were no visions, no clouds, no voice! But I knew that I had to do it. Spurgeon said, 'If you can do anything else, do it.' It is important that one is called.

A fourth assumption is that to be called to the ministry *is an exceedingly high honour*. Do you know which of the tribes of Israel was the most prestigious? It wasn't the tribe of Reuben, Jacob's firstborn; it wasn't the tribe of Judah, through whom Messiah came; it was the tribe of Levi.

This honour was God's reward to them. It goes back to Exodus 32:25,26: 'Moses saw that the people were running wild and that Aaron had let them get out of control and so become a laughing-stock to their enemies. So he stood at the entrance to the camp and said, "Whoever is for the LORD, come to me." And all the Levites rallied to him.' Almost certainly that was the reason why God chose the tribe of Levi to be the vehicle of the ceremonial worship.

The ministry was intended to be respected. It is a different story today. Generally, it would seem that it is those with the least ability and gifts who choose the ministry. But the ministry used to be respected. My father had such a high view of preachers, that it just rubbed off on me. Whenever I see a preacher, I just want to look at him. They are my heroes.

This disrespect common today results in ministers being afraid to preach on certain topics, such as tithing, for their listeners might think they are preaching for their own advantage. I understand that. It is far better that such topics are taught at

home, because if the parents respect the ministry,
then the children will grow up doing the same.

But the Bible does demand respect for those
who serve God:

> Now we ask you, brothers, to respect those who
> work hard among you, who are over you in
> the Lord and who admonish you. Hold them
> in the highest regard in love because of their
> work (1 Thessalonians 5:12-13).

> Obey your leaders and submit to their author-
> ity (Hebrews 13:17).

There are churches where the minister hammers
away at this. The word they use is 'shepherding',
and they stress submission to authority. They go
too far, but we must not ignore the fact that the
Bible does say leaders should be obeyed and their
authority recognized. Leaders should keep watch
over believers, for one future responsibility for
leaders is to give an account to Jesus of their ministry (Hebrews 13:17).

A fifth assumption is that those who minister
were *the Lord's servants*. Several years ago, I was
reading Joshua 1:1 where it says: 'After the death
of Moses the servant of the LORD, the LORD said to
Joshua, the son of Nun, Moses' assistant, "Moses
my servant is dead." ' I thought, 'I wonder if God
would ever say that about me!' I decided right then

that I had rather God feel that way about me than anything else I could think of.

The pilgrims, who would sing this psalm on their way to Jerusalem, recognized that those in the house of the Lord were God's servants. The assumption is that those who go into the ministry are not their own. It is true of all believers, they are bought with a price, but it is even more intense when it comes to the ministry. God intends that there will be a certain standard for the ministry: 'Not many of you should presume to be teachers, my brothers, because you know that we who teach will be judged more strictly' (James 3:1). The ministry should be characterized by a morality that is unquestioned. The exceedingly high honour that is imputed to the ministry must be matched by the fact that those who are called live godly, moral lives.

The ministry and the mandate given to it
The psalm contains a command: 'Praise the LORD, all you servants of the LORD.' The *NIV* is wrong to translate *beraka* as 'praise'; it should be 'bless'. Interestingly, in Psalm 135, where it says 'Praise the LORD' in the *NIV*, a different Hebrew word is used. There it means 'praise'. But the word in Psalm 134 means 'be a blessing to the LORD'. The *NIV* should have left it that way, and oddly enough they did in verse 3: 'May the LORD, the Maker of

heaven and earth, bless you from Zion.'

The point I want to make here is that the Levites, who did their work in the house of the Lord,
were commanded to be a blessing to the Lord. All
believers want to be a blessing to one another. But
the psalmist uses an interesting turn of phrase –
the Levites would be a blessing to the Lord, that's
the idea. The pilgrims gave this mandate to those
who ministered in the temple.

So a minister is to bless the Lord and to be a
blessing to him. Do you know one way in which
you can pray for ministers? Pray that they will be
a blessing to the Lord. An achievable goal is for
ministers to come to the place where their main
desire is to be a blessing to the Lord. I am sorry to
say that I am not there yet, because I care mainly
about being a blessing to other people. But I would
like you to pray that I would be a blessing to the
Lord, that I will be all that he wants me to be. It is
required that stewards be found faithful (1 Corinthians 4:1).

Why did the pilgrims issue this mandate? Some
commentators believe that the pilgrims were singing Psalm 134 as they were going up the steps of
the temple. They had their thoughts on the servants of the Lord in the temple. They prayed for
those in the ministry, because the way the ministry went would determine the way Israel went. If
the priesthood pleased the Lord, then all Israel

would be affected by it and would reap the benefit.

But note the phrase: 'Who minister by night.' I think this means that the minister's task will spring from what he is twenty-four hours a day, especially behind the scenes, when others are sleeping.

Yet we know that there is more to it than that, because in 1 Chronicles 9:33 it says, 'Those who were musicians, heads of Levite families, stayed in the rooms of the temple and were exempt from other duties because they were responsible for the work day and night.' David, who was a musician and singer, took a keen interest in this aspect of the Levitical ceremonial worship. 1 Chronicles 6:31 says, 'These are the men David put in charge of the music in the house of the LORD when the ark came to rest there. They ministered with music before the tabernacle – the Tent of Meeting – until Solomon built the temple of the LORD in Jerusalem. They performed their duties according to the regulations laid down for them.' This was done at night when possibly nobody heard them but the Lord.

That moved me. Imagine going into the house of the Lord and playing instruments and singing, just for the Lord. Isn't that something?

The pilgrims exhorted the Levites to lift up their hands! I have decided that is something God wants me to do more and more. People may think I'm charismatic! Let them think it. There's something beautiful about the practice. The mandate was to be a blessing to the Lord, and it is my view that the lifting up of hands is a blessing to the Lord. I believe it pleases the Lord.

The ministry and the mystery

Why mystery? Because the blessing is reversed. The Levites had been told to be a blessing to the Lord, but now the pilgrims say, 'May the LORD, the Maker of heaven and earth, bless you from Zion.' I'd like to know more of the blessing that comes from the Lord.

What kind of blessing is promised to those who go into the ministry? It is not financial or material blessing. But there are at least two features in the Lord's blessing.

The first is that the minister is blessed spiritually. With an anointing and also with the knowledge that the Lord knows what is happening. I get my greatest comfort from being reminded that the Lord knows. Something can arise that is not right and I don't have anybody I can tell it to. Then I am reminded: he knows.

The second aspect is that all our needs are supplied. The Levites were well taken care of and the church today should ensure that the ministry is looked after with dignity. My first church was in Palmer, Tennessee. My treasurer would say, 'God

will keep you humble and we will keep you poor.'
They were true to their word. But that is not a spirit
that is honouring to God. One can go too far in
one's reaction against the Health and Wealth gospel.

However, ministers must not expect their true
reward on earth but in Heaven. A missionary who
had been in Africa for forty years was going home
to America, and his ship was coming into New
York harbour. On the same ship was President
Theodore Roosevelt, and a band on the pier was
playing for him. Roosevelt had been big game
hunting in Africa, yet when he returned, a band
was playing before gathered crowds. The missionary was by now feeling sorry for himself. But he
went to pray. He said, 'Lord, forty years I've been
serving you, and then one man spends three weeks
in Africa and the band plays for him. He comes
home and look at the welcome he gets.' Then the
Lord said, 'But you're not home yet!'

In the ministry, you may or may not get recognition, respect, blessing or answered prayer, but
one day it will be worth it all. I want so much for
the Lord to say to me, 'Well done!'

R T Kendall is the pastor of Westminster Chapel, London where he is engaged in a much-appreciated Bible teaching ministry. He is a regular speaker at conventions, including Spring Harvest and Keswick.

He has also written over a dozen books and in addition to this book Christian Focus Publications have previously published three of his titles.

Meekness and Majesty deals with the humility of Jesus in his earthly life and the glory of his present heavenly position.

When God Says Well Done urges believers to live so as to please God and be commended by Jesus on the Day of Judgment.

Are You Stone Deaf to the Spirit or Rediscovering God encourages Christians to renew their commitment to Jesus.

For a copy of our current catalogue, please write to

Christian Focus Publications,
Geanies House,
Fearn,
Ross-shire IV20 1TW.